I0532440

Maitreya Sangha

100 copies 2020
Revised and enlarged edition, 100 copies, 2021

© Pentarba Publications

Pentarba.com

3

With reverence and gratitude
We bow to the Teacher,
May the purity of His Teaching remain,
Bringing Joy and the realization of selflessness.
And to the Knights of the Sacred Fire,
Who labor tirelessly to uphold the Cosmic Right.

And to Urusvati, Mother of Agni Yoga,
Illuminating the Way to Infinity.

4

Knights of the Sacred Fire
An Introduction to the Agni Yoga Teachings

With a Glossary of Agni Yoga Terms

Dorje Jinpa

Pentarba Publications

Also by Dorje Jinpa

SENSA: The Lost Language of the Ancient Mysteries

A Synthesis of Alchemy: An Inquiry into the Secrets of Hermetic Philosophy

Essential Teachings of Maitreya: Three Complete Works

Secrets of the Heart: Awakening to Enlightenment

The Book of Hermes

The Coming Avatar: An Essay on the Reappearance of the Christ

Gates to Infinity: A Commentary on the Agni Yoga Infinity Teachings

Available at pentarba.com

He who would swim must dive fearlessly into the water, and he who has dedicated his life to the mastery of Agni Yoga must transform through it his entire life.

*B*y divine right do we affirm the Evolution of Spirit. It is inscribed in our hearts as a living fire. The Path of the Sacred Fire is simple and direct. It leads straight up the rocky crags to the rarefied heights of Infinity. By refining the consciousness in the fire of the heart, we will certainly realize the joy and freedom of the higher worlds. **Precisely, the heart,** says the Teacher, **can open the entrance into the higher worlds. No special asceticism is needed, love, labor and beauty are within the reach of all.**[1]

The Way of the Sacred Fire leads to union with the Divine through the natural affinity that exists between the fire of the heart and the fiery Heart Essence of the Universe. As we embrace this divine Fire our spiritual sensitivity increases, drawing us up, like a magnet, into the higher worlds and the Infinite Oneness of Being.

During the ascent, in courage, firmness, and creativeness, one should remember that the summit itself is small but the horizon is vast. The higher that one ascends the broader and more powerful the vision. The more powerful the vision the stronger is the fusion into oneness.[2]

Striving to the heights is our spiritual destiny. In the same way that a flower naturally turns its face toward the sun, so it is the natural tendency of the human spirit to turn toward the source and essence of it's being. **The heart's joy lies in striving upward.**[3] It is a joy because we are thereby fulfilling

---

[1] *Suvermundane* 812
[2] *Fiery World* III, 19
[3] *Heart* 39

5

our spiritual destiny. The flame of the heart is kindled by striving toward unification with the spiritual world.

There exist no half-measures; there is either striving or the paralyzing cold of death. Moreover, striving is replete with the joy of cosmic realization, whereas the stiffening of death is filled with terror.[1]

We are guided in our ascent by our invisible Guide, invisible to the eyes perhaps, but not to the heart. The heart is our compass, which when magnetized through a close connection with the Guru, will always indicate the correct direction forward.

Whoever ascends will discover that the ascent cannot take place with a heavy load. Furthermore, there is no place on the peak for anything superfluous. The ascending spirit must constantly bear in mind the necessity to break away from the attachments of everyday life.[2] This includes the 'excess baggage' of emotional attachments, beliefs, desires, and habits of thinking, all of which obstruct the path.

The yogas of the past have all stressed the importance of developing nonattachment to earthly possessions. During the crossing into the Subtle World at the death of the body there flashes out all the aspects of the feeling of possession, which troubles even good people. One should assiduously keep in mind this circumstance, and be affirmed upon the realization that earthly possessions do not exist. A great deal has been said about personal possessions, but only the fiery state of consciousness can prove the illusion of the sense of possession. Only when our consciousness remains our sole possession do we feel the freedom of ascent.[3]

During the ascent belief is replaced with direct perception. Emotional entanglements are replaced with the realization of our inseparable unity with all beings. Desire is transmuted into love and wisdom. Habits of thinking are mastered and utilized creatively for the sake of the world.

The nourishment needed to fortify us during our climb will consist of a daily diet of the Teaching,[4] heart felt communion with the Hierarchy, and the absorption of Agni, the Sacred Fire. In direct proportion to our sincere

---

[1] *Agni Yoga* 158.
[2] *Fiery World* III, 19 & 22.
[3] *Fiery World* II, 177
[4] The Agni Yoga Books published by the Agni Yoga Society.

6

upward striving so will be the descent of the Sacred Fire into the Abramram,[1] the fiery Chalice[2] of the Heart. **Humanity nears its sixth stage of perfection, and the flame will soon begin to glow above the Chalice.[3]**

 Ram

Abram

The gifts of the Higher Forces are gathered in the chalice and given from the chalice.[4] When we are told to be careful not to spill the chalice it means to not carelessly squander our store of psychic energy. In the initiation ceremonies of many cultures the chalice is raised 'above the head' as an offering to the Supreme. When we say, **"Accept my heart oh Lord, and sacrifice it for the sake of the world,"[5]** we are offering our precious psychic energy to the Spiritual Hierarchy of Masters to be used as needed for the sake of the world.

When you hear the word Abramram, it will be a reminder about the center of the Chalice, where straight-knowledge predestined for the future evolution is concentrated. When you hear about 'fiery wings,' it will mean the centers of the shoulders. Likewise, the 'treasures of the five summits' will be the centers of Brahmarandhra, the wrists, and the knees. When a sudden weakness is felt under the knees, or a strain in the wrists, this will mean the sharpening of the Brahmarandhra.[6] The Brahmarandhara center, the twelve petaled heart lotus at the crown of the head, has been called the Nirvana Chakra.[7] The Fire of Life descends into the Chalice, where as depicted in the symbolism of Aquarius, it is freely given as needed for the sake of the world.

The light of the Chalice kindles the rainbow of radiance!

---

[1] Abram is the chalice and Ram is the seed syllable for fire. See Glossary.
[2] See Glossary
[3] *Agni Yoga* 553. The 'sixth stage' is the Sixth Race.
[4] *The Fiery World* III, 49
[5] *Leaves of Morys's Garden I,* 317
[6] *Agni Yoga* 596
[7] See *The Philosophy of Gorakhnath* by Akshaya Banerjea, page 179

The Teacher will point out the path to the freedom of the Higher Worlds but he will not take us there. Every step must be taken under our own power, on our own initiative, and of our own free will. We are guided and encouraged, but we are not compelled to remove the chains of ignorance. We are told of the divine spark of wisdom, love, and creative power hidden within us, but we are not compelled to embrace it.

The Way of the Sacred Fire is intended for those few **who recognizes that his knowledge is insignificant, who seldom thinks of the distinctions bestowed upon him by others, who has not taken part in any wrong doings of religions, who, remembering about reincarnation, does not overvalue his earthly bloodline, who can yearly repeat the planting of his garden, smiling at the storms that undid his past labors, who has lost the ability to slander, who has aimed his striving search toward the invisible Supreme, who has rejected the companionship of all betrayers of truth, and who has encircled himself with purity of thinking, which produces an invincible aura** of benevolence.

Who then are my people? Those who do not feel any place to be their home; those who do not attach any value to objects; who love to ascend mountains; who love the singing of birds; who value the air of the morning hour; who value action more than time; who understand flowers; who display fearlessness without noticing it; who abhor gossip; who esteem the manifestation of the joy of beauty; who understand the life beyond the limits of the visible; who feel when one can partake of amrita;[1] who hasten to fulfill the prophecy. These are my people. They can use my power.[2]

According to Master M, the Kali-Yuga, the age of darkness and ignorance, is now coming to an end. This has been verified by the remarkable seer Rudolf Steiner.[3] The forces of darkness are therefore fighting hard to resist the incoming light of the new Satya Yuga, the age of truth and light. **Anyone who knows about the approaching end of the Kali Yuga**

---

[1] Divine elixir.
[2] *Leaves of Morya's Garden II, 288*
[3] See his *Karmic Relationships*, Volume 3, chapter 6.

8

understands that it cannot occur without world upheavals. The forces that were particularly powerful during the 'Black Age' must now struggle for survival. They prefer a general catastrophe to defeat.[1]

Before the great reorganization of the world, a manifestation of all the dark forces is displayed, for a better transmutation. What is taking place in the world cannot be called a step of evolution; what is being manifested is the lowest, the most intense, the most saturated by the forces of darkness.... The stage that the planet is going through can be compared with a furnace of Cosmic Fire. Thus the World is being reconstructed by the tension of two polarities.[2]

We are at a time of great transition, upheaval, and a shifting of the energies. The darkest hour, it is said, is just before the dawn.

There is an ancient prophecy concerning this time, given by Gautama Buddha and preserved in the archives of the great Kalachakra Tradition. It says that at the end of the Kali-Yuga, the Avatar Rigden Drapo[3] will descend from the celestial kingdom of Shamballa to lead His Fiery Warriors into battle against the forces of darkness. **One should gather all unwaveringness of the heart in order to find oneself in the ranks of Rigden.**[4]

---

[1] *Supermundane 127*
[2] *Fiery World* III, 167
[3] Also spelled Jyepo, Djapo, Djyepo.
[4] *Heart* # 380

Rigden, the Coming Avatar, is also known as Kalki, Rudra Chakrin, and the Avatar of Synthesis.[2] He stands closely with the Teacher, the author of the Agni Yoga Books, who in Theosophical literature is known as Master Morya. In the Matsya Purana,[3] an ancient Hindu scripture, Morya is called Maru,[4] also spelled Moru, a great Sage of the Maurya lineage, who is said to be still living in the Himalayan Mountains, and who will, according to this scripture, come forth at the beginning of the Krita Yuga to reestablish the reign of the Kshattriya, the Warrior Kings, the lineage of the 'divine right of kings.' Krita Yuga is another name for the Satya Yuga, the Age of Truth, which is to begin shortly. Edwin Bernbaum in his book *The Way to Shamballa* writes: "In the *Kalki Purana*, a sage King named Maru [Morya], a descendant of an earlier incarnation of Vishnu, lives there in the Himalayas, awaiting the end of the age of discord [Kali Yuga]. When Kalki [the coming avatar] comes to liberate the world, this sage will join him in the final battle against the barbarians. After their victory over the forces of evil, Maru will gain a throne

---

[1] Rigden Jyepo by Nichols Roerich.
[2] See my *The Coming Avatar*, Pentarba Publications, Pentarba.com
[3] Chapter CCIXXII.
[4] According to the *Secret Doctrine* Maru is a corruption of Morya. Max Muller translated the name as Morya, of the Morya Dynasty. See *The Secret Doctrine* by H. P. Blavatsky, Adyar Edition, Vol. 2., page 93.

and assist Kalki in establishing a golden age."[1] A similar prophecy can be found in the *Vishnu Purâna*[2] where it is stated that there was in the Sorya Dynasty a king called "Maru, who, through the power of yoga, is still living in the village called Kalapa. In a future age he will be the restorer of the Kshatriya race in the solar dynasty." According to H. P. Blavatsky, "the Kshatriya is a race of Warrior Kings."[3] In the great *Bhagavata Purana* it is stated that the Kalki Avatar will appear "when the present Kali Yuga is about to end. With Him will appear Maru and his Brother Devapi, who, at the end of the Kali Yuga, will reestablish the schools that teach Varnas [classes of people, the Rays] and Stamas [stages of the path, the Initiations] and will reestablish the reign of the Kshatriyas Kings, that came to an end at the beginning of the Kali Yuga."[4] The schools that are to be reestablished are the ancient Mystery Schools.

The above image is a detail from a painting by the Tibetan Adept Gai Ben-Jamin, magically precipitated on silk for H.P. Blavatsky at her request, showing Morya on horseback at His home in the Himalayas. Ben-Jamin has

---

[1] Pages 83-84.

[2] Book IV, Chapter 4

[3] First Ray. See H.P. Blavatsky Collected Writings Vol. VI, page 40-41.

[4] Skandhi 12: 2kast. The *Mahabharata* is the story of how Krishna came to earth to greatly reduce the power of the Kshatriyas, the cast of the warrior kings, before the beginning of the Age of Kali.

11

been identified as Djwhal Khul, the Abbott of a large monastery on the borders of Tibet. Helena and Nicholas Roerich, during their expedition through Tibet, visited Djwal Khul at his monastery near Darjeeling.[1] The original precipitated painting on Chinese silk is housed at the Theosophical Headquarters at Adyar.

The Fiery Warriors are often called by this name because Satya Yuga begins with the approach of the element of Fire. Those who gather at this time are imbued with this penetrating element…. The East knows of the Army of Fiery Warriors that will arise before the coming of the New Era.[2] The New Era begins amidst thunder and Lightening…[3]

Nicholas Roerich, while visiting the Chum Monastery, was told: "The time of the great advent is nearing and according to our prophecies the Epoch of Shambhala has already begun. Rigden Japo, the ruler of Shambhala, is already preparing his unconquerable army for the last fight. All his assistants and officers are already incarnating."[4]

The Knights of the Sacred Fire gather together under the banner of the Spiritual Hierarchy, Masters of Wisdom, Bodhisattvas, Rishis, call them what you will, who guard and guide the spiritual evolution of the world. **Every belief reveals the Guarding Angles, Guides, and Comforters; under the various names lies the same concept of Hierarchy. Verily, let each one understand in their own way, but let each heart strive upwards. In this alone is the path to perfection.[5]**

The spiritual Hierarchy, the Elder Brothers of the race, graduates of the school of life on the earth, are the source of the ageless wisdom as taught in the ancient schools of Mystery. **Like milestones on a luminous path, the Brothers of Humanity, ever alert, are standing guard, ready to lead the**

---

[1] "When we manifest ourselves we cannot be distinguished from other people. You yourselves can testify that when Djwal Khul came to welcome you He appeared no different from the other Lamas. Urusvati immediately sensed something unusual, but this feeling could have been caused similarly by the head of the monastery." *Supermundane 40*.
[2] *Agni Yoga* 307
[3] *Agni Yoga* 277
[4] *Abode of Light* by Nicholas Roerich, page 74.
[5] *AUM* 60

traveler into the chain of ascent.[1] They provide the inner guidance for those pilgrims on the Way, regardless of their religious affiliations. In ancient times they were known to every nation. And while at the present time, after centuries of the Kali Yuga and the darkness of materialism, they have been nearly forgotten, traces of their existence can still be found preserved, under different names, in the esoteric traditions of many cultures.

The Mahayana Buddhists call them Bodhisattvas, those enlightened Arhats who have renounced the highest nirvana in order to remain in cyclic existence (samsara) to help liberate all sentient beings from suffering. The Community of Bodhisattvas (*Sangha*) is one of the three esoteric Jewels of Buddhism, along with the Buddha, esoterically representing the Buddha Nature, the spiritual essence within all beings, and the Dharma, the Path described in the Buddha's teaching.

In the Bible they are known as the Cloud of Witnesses, the Watchers, and the Elders who surround the throne of God. The esoteric school established by St. Paul in Athens, spoke of them as the Celestial Hierarchy.[2] Origen, the most enlightened of the early Christian Fathers, called them the Sons of Resurrection. The Catholic Church speaks of the Communion of Saints who assist the weary pilgrims. To Enoch they were the holy Sons of God—"And it came to pass that my spirit was transformed and it ascended into the heavens. And I saw the holy Sons of God. Their garments were white and their faces shown like snow."

In the Greek Mysteries they were called Daemons, "invisible powers that act as intermediaries between the Gods and the souls of men, and who always follow the will of the Gods"[3] The Gods of the Greek Mysteries are primarily Planetary and Solar Deities, and should not to be confused with the mythological gods as portrayed in the Olympian allegories. Pythagoras referred to the Hierarchy as Muses and 'Celestial Heros.' To the Sufis they were "the invisible Hierarchy of Watchers, awakened ones who live in the Celestial Earth, the future home of those who conquer." In the Mysteries they were the Hierophants, the Initiators and Guardians of the Secrets. To

---

[1] *Hierarchy* Preface
[2] See Dionysius of Aeropagite, *Celestial Hierarchy* & *Ecclesiastical Hierarchy.*
[3] *On the Mysteries of the Egyptians, Chaldeans, and Assyrians by* Iamblichus,

13

the Masons, who have their roots in the Ancient Mysteries, they were known as the Accepted Masters of the Blue Lodge of the Heavens (Sirius). The Theosophists called them Masters of Wisdom. The Hindus speak of the immortal Rishis who gave to the world the Revelation of the Vedas. To the ancient Chinese Taoists they were the Dragons of Wisdom and Immortals, for they had conquered death. The ancient Egyptians called them 'Guardians of the Light.' And in modern times they have become known as the Great White Brotherhood. At the beginning of each of the Agni Yoga Books they are named in Tibetan script—*The Maitreya Sangha*, the Ashram of Maitreya, the head of the Hierarchy of Bodhisattvas.

The Brothers of Humanity willingly renounce Paranirvana for the affirmation of the evolution of the human spirit.[1] At great personal sacrifice the Brothers remain in the three worlds of samsara for the sake of humanity and the world, leaving for a future time those higher states and dimensions of Being that calls to them.

What is the nature of the Bodhisattvas' compassion? Without coercing the will, they invisibly and patiently direct each suitable force toward good. It is not difficult to conduct oneself according to the guidance of the Bodhisattvas, for all characteristics of the spirit are allowed for by them.[2]

The Great Brotherhood, the Ashram of Maitreya, has no physical organization, though it is said that they will soon reestablish the Mysteries, the schools of initiation on earth. And while the Hierarchy directs its creative activity from subtle planes, it has many coworkers, in and out of incarnation, who labor to hasten the divine Plan.

The term 'God' is seldom used in the Teaching. The reason for this lies not in a denial of a Supreme Being, but rather that the old-world meaning of the term no longer applies. The God idea must now be broadened to include

---

[1] *Hierarchy* 1
[2] *Agni Yoga* 332

14

the Infinite Synthesis or Oneness of Being manifesting through an infinite ever-ascending Hierarchy of Spiritual Beings. **The concept of God in all its grandeur is clarified on the basis of Hierarchy. Only thus can the highest concept emerge from abstraction and blend with all existence.**[1]

The Hierarchy is our essential nature, the very essence of out being. What the Atma, or Christos, or Buddha Nature is for a human being, Hierarchy is for humanity. **Blessed is he who realizes in his heart the essential reality of Hierarchy.**[2] **The very quality of life, the actual realization of the path, has been founded on successiveness, as an extension into Infinity . . . The magnitude of Hierarchy extends into Infinity.**[3]

Let words about the Lords resound in all corners of the world. They are candles lit before the holy shrines. They are lamps of Living Fire—a protection against all diseases.[4]

Agni is the oldest and most esteemed of the Gods of India. In the *Bhagavata Purana* he is said to represent, "The sacred Fire hidden at the heart of all beings."[5] **Each of us carries within himself the One Fire, immutable throughout the entire universe. No one cares to imagine that the universal treasure is within him.**[6]

Throughout the Agni Yoga Teaching the term Fire (Agni) represents the one Primordial Energy in all its gradations. The Sacred Fire manifests in the human kingdom as psychic energy, the creative power of thought. This includes the creative power of thought, the fire of the heart, and the electromagnetic energy of the ethereal body. Yoga is a Sanskrit term meaning to unite. Agni Yoga, therefore, is the path that leads to union with the divine through the refinement and application of psychic energy. A strong store of refined psychic energy is called *Virya*, one of the Six-Perfections taught by

---

[1] *Fiery World* II 188
[2] *Fiery World* II 289.
[3] *Fiery World* II 290
[4] *Fiery World* I 10
[5] Skandha 7:11
[6] *Fiery World* I # 7

15

the Buddha. **Agni Yoga is the perception and application in life of the all-embracing element of Fire, which nourishes the seed of the spirit.**[1]

As a fundamental principle Fire (Energy) is the Essence, the essential nature of all manifested life. This is born out to some degree by Albert Einstein who says that matter is really nothing but energy vibrating at the speed of light squared ($e=mc^2$). This famous equation can, of course, be applied equally well to the psychic realm, "As above, so below." The substances of thought (chitta), for example, are psychic energies vibrating at different degrees of intensity and refinement.

Psychic energy, like all energies, is dual—creative and receptive, electric and magnetic. The creative aspect of psychic energy is the power of thought. Its receptive nature is the fire of the heart, the fire that illuminates the consciousness. To perceive with pure spiritual sensitivity and to create through the power of though are both manifestations of psychic energy. **That a situation is without solution is only imagined by those who would rely on other people rather than upon the power of their own thoughts.**

Thought is creative! The power of thought stimulates what ever it focuses its attention upon. The quality of the thought depends upon the feelings that saturate it. **The power of thought depends upon calmness and heart-striving. This should always be kept in mind, because people too often place the will in the brain.**[2] Heart felt striving for unity with the Hierarchy, for example, miraculously establishes that unity. Striving creates according to the clarity of thought and the quality of the feeling behind it. When labor is emphasized in the Teaching it refers primarily to the creative application of the subtle energy of thought and feeling to further the evolution of consciousness, in oneself and in the world. While this can manifest as physical labor, it is primary the creative activity of the mind, colored by the receptive subtle energy of the heart that is the labor of the Knights of the Sacred Fire.

And how should we approach the sacred Fire? **Purify your thoughts, and after determining your three worst traits, sacrifice them to be burned in**

---

[1] *Agni Yoga* 185
[2] *Brotherhood* 546

fiery striving. Then choose a teacher on earth. Mastering the Teaching. Strength your body with the indicated medicines and pranayama. You will behold the stars of the spirit. You will see the flames of purification of your centers. You will hear the voice of the invisible Teacher. And you will acquire those subtlest perceptions that transform life.[1]

The 'indicated medicines' include valerian root, which should be taken every evening as a tea or tincture. It strengthens the nerves and the nerve centers. Phosphorous, found in baking soda, and eucalyptus oil and deodar resin are also useful medicines . The 'stars of spirit' are one of the first signs of Agni Yoga. They appear unexpectedly in one's field of vision as sparks of colored light, often of electric blue or white. They indicate the activity of fire. The voice of the Teacher may manifest as a clap of thunder or as the gentlest touch, but it will always carry the same heart felt signature even in a reprimand. Rarely more than a single word or thought is give.

The practice of Agni Yoga includes: **Prayer and inner concentration[2]** (meditation). This includes silent communion, with love and readiness, with the Teacher or the Hierarchy, without words or extraneous thoughts. For this an image of the Teacher is useful for focus.[3] This meditation can be long or short but should be for at least 10 minutes.

A short simple pranayama in the morning is useful. This should not become a fetish as **there is nothing more dangerous as too much energy.**

Let us regard the relation between the Teacher and disciple. The Teacher gives indications within those limits permitted. He uplifts the disciple, cleansing him of the outworn habits. He warns him against all kinds of treason, superstition and hypocrisy. He tries the disciple openly and in secret. The Teacher unbars the gates of the next step with the words, 'Rejoice brother.' He may also close them with the words, 'Farewell, passerby.'[4]

The disciple chooses his own Teacher. He reveres him as one of the highest beings. He trusts him and brings him his best thoughts. He cherishes the name of the Teacher and inscribes it upon the glaive of his

---

[1] *Agni Yoga* 185. Also see *The Science of Breath* by Ramacharaka
[2] *AUM 4*
[3] See *Hierarchy*
[4] *Agni Yoga* 103

17

sword. He shows diligence in labor and flexibility in achievement. He meets trials as the light of the morning and directs his hope to the lock of the next gates.

Friends, if you wish to approach us, elect a teacher on earth and place in him your guidance. He will tell you in time when the key may be turned in the gates. Each one should have a teacher on earth.[1]

The importance of the relationship between the student and his or her earthly teacher should not be underestimated or approached lightly. Choose a teacher with heart, for it is only through the heart that unity is achieved. The teacher should be tested. The display of negative emotions, for example, is a sure indication that you should to seek elsewhere, for it means that the first steps of yoga have not yet been realized. The charging of money for spiritual instruction, may also be cause to look elsewhere. **Do not listen to the teacher who demands a fee for his teaching.[2]**

In the West there have appeared many self-proclaimed yogis, magicians, hypnotists, and occultists, who make phenomena produced by the will. Brilliantly multiplying their coins, they teach people, for a fee, how to improve their material condition; how to induce others to trust them; how to win influence in society; how to gain success in business; how to compel others to obey their orders; how to turn life into a rose garden. In teaching others to develop the will, some of these teachers may seem to be following a good path, but because they do not indicate any goal in this journey, they serve only to worsen the already ugly conditions of life.[3] The great Sufi saint Hazarat Inyat Khan has given us an excellent way to recognize the false teachers: 'They are the ones beating the drum.' Look for signs of egotism and pride. Do they display a picture of themselves on the covers of their books? Do they speak about their experiences of enlightenment? Do not fall into the trap of believing that popularity is an indication of attainment. The reverse is more often the case.

A worthy teacher will also test the student's sincerity, steadfastness, and courage. Can constructive criticism be accepted without irritation? Does

---

[1] *Agni Yoga* 103
[2] *Agni Yoga*, 93
[3] *Agni Yoga, 404*

18

the student speak ill of others behind their backs? A probation period is usual. When you have formally asked and have been accepted by a spiritual teacher certain energies are set in motion that are harmful to both parties to latter disconnect in a negative way. The teacher, in accepting a student, assumes thereby a certain degree of responsibility for the student's progress, a responsibility that often continues into future lives. In this the laws of karma are particularly potent on both sides. Turning against one's teacher, even in thought, is a heinous crime with severe repercussions.

Through a physical plane teacher the student can receive specific instructions pertaining to their particular situation and station on the path. **In the methods of Yoga it is impossible to apply the same means for all. And yet, quite often in lectures and discourses general methods are mentioned, and those present are deluded into thinking that the prescription is for one and all. Only a very attentive scrutiny of the spiritual condition of the individual in question will give the right guidance to the indications for him.**[1]

A worthy teacher will guide the students spiritually, but will seldom instruct in personal matters relating to family, friends, and lovers. This is left to the student. The teacher will make suggestion, but will not command, coerce, or in any way interfere with the student's free will.

To those who declare the wish to dispense with a guide or teacher, commend them for realizing the need for self-reliance and independent thinking, but at the same time ask them if they have really penetrated so deeply in the Way that they no longer need a guide. This is unlikely. The more we refine and expand the consciousness the greater is our realization of how vast, unknown, and treacherous is the way ahead. The traps, pitfalls, illusions, and enticing dead-ends are numerous. The farther we advance the greater will be the attacks of the enemy. Without a powerful and wise Friend to help us our chances have been likened to **a kitten at sea**. All the masters are disciples of greater masters, ad infinitum. This is the foundation of the Chain of Hierarchy.

Of course the best teacher will always emphasize independent thinking, the need to learn from experience, to realize the truth first hand for oneself

---

[1] *Fiery World* 1, 127

and not to rely on authority, even the authority of the Teacher for one's perception of the truth. But having a teacher and learning from experience are not contradictory concepts. Both are needed. **Some people must memorize useful counsels whereas others know the fundamentals of life in their hearts; both kinds need a teacher.**[1]

The purpose of spiritual reading is to awaken the fire of spiritual vision deep within us. Reading spiritual books to accumulate knowledge is secondary and can even become harmful when crystalized into a fixed religious dogma. **Flexibility of consciousness is needed so as not to crystallize the Teaching into a fixed dogma.**[1] So in this we must learn to distinguish between the spirit of the law and the letter of the law. The letter of the law leads to conflict, sectarian divisions, and a fixation of view, preventing further progress. The spirit of the law illuminates the consciousness.

The Agni Yoga Teaching is offered in such a way as to awaken the fiery heart essence within us. It contains few dogmatic assertions for the rational mind to fixate upon. The Teaching is not an intellectual treatise, but rather a book of hints, which when applied, will awaken spiritual insight and will.

Studying the Teaching broadens not only the consciousness of the student, it saturates space with spiritual truth, thus making it available psychically to those seeking the truth.

The purpose of the Teaching, as a catalyst for yoga (spiritual union), is greater than the mere accumulation of information. First it provides a connection with the Author, with Hierarchy. Secondly it opens the consciousness to new and expanded way of perception. By thinking about what we read we attract rare vibrations of a corresponding nature. It is these spiritual vibrations that elevates and transforms the consciousness. When we think about the Teacher, for example, we open ourselves to a portion of his exalted vibrations. Spiritual vibrations, which descend from above, are in fact Agni (all pervading primary Energy). When terms like higher and lower are

---

[1] *Fiery World* I # 516.
[1] *Heart* 193

20

use in esoteric literature they do not refer to directions of space, but rather to rates of vibration.

Find a way to make the Teaching a part of your everyday life. The busiest people can devote an hour to the Teaching. We cannot believe that there is not a moment available for the most essential for that for which we live. Daily we partake of food and without it regard the day as miserable. But our spirit also requires nourishment of thought, and it is a crime to pass one's day without it.

The Teaching offers perfection as the goal; without this it would have no future. The Teaching pays no attention to personal comfort; otherwise it would be egotism. The Teaching advocates the beautifying of existence, which otherwise would submerge in ugliness. The Teaching is always self-denying, because it knows the true meaning of the Common Good. The Teaching reveres knowledge; otherwise it would be darkness. The Teaching is manifested in life not through invented ceremonies, but on the basis of experience. I consider that the way of the Teaching has nothing to do with the husks of outworn ways.[1]

The Teaching is presented according to that ancient esoteric tradition that veils the hidden meaning of many passages behind abbreviations, unusual wording, poetic and symbolic expressions. One of the reasons for this is that by striving to understand the hidden meaning spiritual insight is awakened, the consciousness is expanded, and the imparted truths become, not something memorized from a book, but something realized directly. What was at first incomprehensible, is eventually understood through focused attention. Thus, the daily reading and contemplation of the Teaching is a primary spiritual exercise. Spiritual insight, which in the Teaching is called straight-knowledge, is developed only through igniting the unifying fire of the heart. The Teaching is therefore protected from those who lack heart sensitivity, for they will not understand the deeper implications. The Teaching does not require great intellectual ability. It requires the awakening of a fiery sensitivity.

When beginning the Teaching many passages will not be understood. Do not let this stop you. Many of the verses, not grasped upon the surface,

---

[1] *Agni Yoga*, 404

will nevertheless penetrate to deeper levels of the subconscious mind. Human beings are fragmented in their consciousness. The highest and best aspects are hidden from view. The object of yoga is the unification of the consciousness.

The Teaching is presented on many levels so that everyone can find information appropriate to their level of attainment. By presenting ideas ahead of our present understanding, it causes us to strive to broaden the scope of our consciousness. It is by striving that our ability to understand will be realized. Veiling the Teaching, also weeds out the curious, the lazy minded, and those who would only harm themselves and others by a premature exposure to a teaching that they cannot yet safely put into practice.

The Teaching is also veiled so as to not infringe upon the free will or karma of the student. **You may have noted in my words cryptic passages or separate words not clear for today. Remember guidance is on the condition that karma be not infringed upon.**[1] If the Teacher is too explicit, gives too much help, or makes it too easy, it can becomes a kind of compulsion, forcing the weak willed into the Light without personal effort, feelings of responsibility, or conscious decision. This, we are told, always leads to disaster. It is inadmissible to interfere with the free will of another, except perhaps in the defense of family and friends.

While the Teaching does assumes a certain degree of intelligence on the part of the student, it is not so much the rational mind that is needed, but rather a broad experienced consciousness, a spiritual sensitivity that is saturated, uplifted, and refined by feelings of the heart. The Teaching is also veiled to protect the Teaching itself from distortion. We need only examine the many interpretations of the Christian scriptures to see how dangerous distortions of the sacred texts can be.

It is a fundamental law of Nature that pure striving will attract from deep within the consciousness the necessary understanding. **Whoever wishes he will understand!**

Ponder to what extent you can understand my language and express it in your own tongue. Similarly understand your reciprocal feelings and

---

[1] *Leaves of Morya's Garden* II page 145

express them in the language of the heart. This language will open the gates to Infinity.[1] For a true understanding of the Teaching it must be given a careful and thoughtful reading. To help in this we are asked to watch closely our response to the Teaching to see how much of its language is being understood. We are then asked to express that understanding in our own words paying particular attention to the feelings that arise from this understanding, and allowing these feelings of the heart to work upon us in such a way that it merges fully with the consciousness. It is useful to consider the Teaching as a book of seed-thoughts for meditation.

By putting the Teaching in our own words we not only aid the assimilation process, but it will also saturate space with ideas that will lead to the New World. If the thoughts are clear and sounded with pure intention who knows how many lives will be benefited. Stating the Teaching in our own words also helps to make the given truths our own. We are striving for insight not book learning.

To read and contemplate the Teaching while walking in nature helps to establish a rhythm of thought that is helpful for assimilation. Another way to help establish a rhythm is to practice at the same hour every morning (preferably at dawn). As stated in the Teaching, prearranged dates attract like a magnet corresponding energies from space at the designated hour.

It is also useful in our reading of the Teaching to begin at the beginning, or at least reading the books you are attracted to straight through from the beginning. The reason for this is that the Teaching contains a beautiful rhythmic magnetism that works on subtle levels. The Teacher advises the student not to skip around so that the rhythm of the inner transmission is not interrupted. **By tracing the sequence of the Teaching one can see the turns of an ascending spiral. Such curving is effected in order that humanity be imperceptibly moved forward. Just as we cannot perceive the extent of growth of grass each instant, so too, each new turn of the spiral does not register in the consciousness.**[2]

It is not enough to simply read and absorb the ideas presented, they must be applied in life, consciously and with decision. In this way its truths

---

[1] *Infinity 1 Preamble*
[2] *AUM 273*

become verified through direct experience. One of the primary ways in which the Teaching can be applied in life is to embrace the ideas presented fully in the consciousness. **Can one presume that the Teaching has been applied in life if even one's thoughts have not received a new impetus? Do not seek for new seedlings where all remains as before. Where the old dominates, the new Fire will scorch and life will not receive its new blessing.**[1]

The Teaching comes to life when it is linked with its source.[2] The bond with the Teacher transforms the Teaching into a living spiritual current. The Teaching is often given in a highly abbreviated, form. A close connection with the consciousness of invisible Teacher will supply the missing pieces.

The Teaching must not be interpreted in a fixed dogmatic fashion. For example, when the Teacher warns us against the dangers of magic this does not include the miraculous achievements made through the application of psychic energy, such as levitation, moving objects with the mind, seeing the future, etc. The magic that we are warned against primarily pertains to unnaturally invoking energies and entities from the elemental world.[3] And when the Teaching speaks of the horrors of psychism and mediumism (astral channeling) this does not include hearing the voice of the Teacher or communicating with coworkers at a distance. There are many such examples where statements of truth must not be turned into a fixed dogma. To help prevent this it is wise to study other world religions, yogas, and philosophies. **One can understand and apply the Agni Yoga Teachings only after having been in touch with other Teachings of Life.**[4] The world religions all have a common source. They approach the same higher truths, but from the perspective of their own time and culture. But even this should not be taken in the extreme. Not all paths and philosophies lead to the goal. **The broadening of consciousness was stressed long ago, but it is still misunderstood. People often believe that the broadening of consciousness is simply the acceptance**

---

[1] *Agni Yoga* 341
[2] *Supermundane* I, 60
[3] See *Agni Yoga* 233
[4] *Agni Yoga* 295

of everything, but then the consciousness would be turned into a cheap roadside inn![1]

The Way of the Sacred Fire is marked with a love of the beautiful. This love draws the yogi like a magnet to all that is beautiful, even to the root source of beauty itself. It is incorrect to say that beauty is subjective and therefore relates only to the individual. Beauty is a universal principle that the eye of the beholder either perceives or not. Beauty is our destiny, the equilibrium and perfection of the Way. It is our mission in life to create beauty. **He is no sower in the field of creation who feels no tremor in the realization that he creates beauty.**[2] The love of the beautiful opens the yogi to ananda, great joy. **People have only two real joys—thinking and the ecstasy over beauty.**[3]

When our sensitivity to the beauty of higher truth has been awakened the Teaching takes on new significance. In this way the magnetic power of spiritual attraction increases and the union of joy and understanding becomes a spontaneous expression. **Be aflame with beauty!**[4] Thus the perception of beauty becomes an accurate guide to the upward way and to those acts of creativeness that are in step with evolution. **The closest to perfection will be the path of beauty.**[5]

The attractive power of the beautiful is one of the primary motivating impulses of the creative spirit. **Those who live under the power of beauty are attracted toward construction. They create by their potentiality the mastery of spirit. They regenerate life through beauty. But terrible is the life of those who live by the power of destruction! Of course, speaking of the power of destruction, one should have in mind the power of selfhood, which is opposed to the power of beauty. Thus one should understand clearly that a man either casts himself into an abyss or is uplifted into Infinity.**[6]

---

[1] *Supermundane* 521.
[2] *Aum,* 300
[3] *Brotherhood 85*
[4] *Fiery World* 410
[5] *Fiery World* III, 31
[6] *Fiery World* III, 28

Only a sense of beauty can lead to synthesis.[1] Beauty is the unification of complimentary energies whose activity is balanced and harmonious. If we can perceive this principle holistically, we may be able to realize the reality of synthesis as beauty raised to it's highest most exalted level of being. Beauty, which is attained when the Middle Way between the two extremes is known and followed, leads to the realization of the Synthesis.

*W*herein lies the success of a yogi? It is not the attraction of crowds, not the conversion of the multitudes. But near the works of the yogi, one can observe how others emulate him. Consciously or unconsciously, voluntarily or involuntarily, people begin to do the same thing. Even his enemies, while cursing him, are drawn in his wake. It is as if a special atmosphere had gathered about the action of the yogi. This is true success, when neither money nor fame, but the invisible fire kindles human hearts.[2]

You may be asked how the entrance upon the path of service is defined. Certainly the first sign will be renunciation of the past and full striving to the future.

The second sign will be the realization of the Teacher within one's heart, not because it is necessary thus, but because it is impossible otherwise.

The third sign will be the rejection of fear, for being armed by the Lord one is invulnerable.

The forth will be non-condemnation, because he who strives into the future has no time to occupy himself with the refuse of yesterday.

The fifth will be the filling of the entire time with labor for the future.

The sixth will be the joy of service and completely offering oneself for the good of the world.

The seventh will be spiritual striving to the far-off worlds as a predestined path.[3]

Our thoughts have the creative power of psychic energy behind them. To look forward moves us forward. To dwell on the past moves us back.

---

[1] *Agni Yoga* 302
[2] *Agni Yoga* 375
[3] *Hierarchy* 196

26

The harm of condemnation and negative gossip, particularly when created in group formation, cannot be over stated. The one condemned is certainly harmed; but the greatest harm is in the inevitable returning blow.

Through communion with Hierarchy the attainment of illumination, spiritual intuition, becomes possible. This should not, however, be confused with 'being psychic.' The second hand information derived from psychism (channeling) may be true and useful, but usually it arises from the astral plane, the home of the collective subconscious with all of its deceptive emotions and desires. **Psychism is a window into the subtle World, but the teacher tells the pupil, 'Do not turn so often to the window. Look directly into the Book of Life.'[1]**

Opened centers are symptoms of right development, but with them comes the danger of mediumism. A medium is but an inn for disembodied liars.[2] Spiritual striving plus an expanded and refined consciousness opens the centers (chakras). This greatly increases the yogi's sensitivity to the unseen world and his ability to here the voices of disembodied entities of all kinds, higher and lower. **Beings existing in subtle bodies of different levels can direct thoughts to those on Earth. Uniting with the highest can open a path to the lowest.** Be careful, watch your thoughts.

Much has already been said about psychism, nevertheless this scourge of humanity is insufficiently understood. Psychism blunts each aspiration, and higher attainment remains inaccessible. The sphere of activity of a man engulfed by psychism is limited within a charmed circle in which all the energies that retard growth of the spirit find their fitting place. Psychism embraces the manifestation of the lowest energies, and the fires of the centers are extinguished by these precipitations. With psychism there is inevitably to be found disorder of the nervous system. In addition, the breaking away from vital functions closes the path to self-perfection. Creativeness is blunted, and there is established a passive state which makes a man an instrument for the influx of all kinds of forces. By reason of

---

[1] *Fiery World* II. 14. Also see Fiery World III. 309.
[2] *Agni Yoga 228*

27

relaxation of the will, control is weakened, and by this the attraction of various lower entities is increased.[1]

We must not automatically assume that thoughts appearing in our mind-stream are our own or come form a high source. **Even senior disciples have been fooled.** We do receive inspiration and guidance from Hierarchy, of course, and once in a great while, when necessary for the work, even a word or two is given. But inspiration from the Hierarchy is accompanied by exaltation and joy. Even a reprimand will carry at its foundation a high vibration.

Precisely, psychism and mediumism turn man away from the Higher Spheres, for the subtle body becomes thus so saturated with lower emanations that the entire being is altered.

The enemies who uplift the sword are not so dangerous as those who penetrate under the mask of light.[2]

We are not at all pleased to see that intercourse with the lower spheres is increasing.[3] At a certain level of attainment the Knights of the Sacred Fire, who labor for the common good, all will experience negative thoughts and emotions that originate from outside their own sphere of activity. Through close vigilant observation we can learn to distinguish these thoughts from the ravings of our own subconscious mind.

Parents would like to protect their children from the madness, chaos and darkness of the times. But they soon realize that overprotection creates weaklings. The Hierarchy of Masters understand this truth. Often they will stand aside thus allowing the spiritual warriors to develop their fiery skills through first hand experience. **We value those fighters who bravely repel the assaults of darkness.**

We are guarded on all paths. The manifested protection descends from above, but let us also provide our own shield against earthly arrows.[4]

Be assured, we are protected from the forces of darkness! But we are not protected from ourselves. We must experience fully the karmic effects of those negative living thought forms we have created that always return to

---

[1] *Fiery World III*, 309
[2] *Fiery World* III, 165
[3] *Fiery World* I, 632
[4] *Supermundane* 512

their creator to be transmuted. **The Teacher can protect to a certain degree, but the shadow dance of the past will continue its round.**[1] Also there comes a time when, as a part of the necessary process of self-mastery, the student warrior must learn to repel unwanted guests themselves. The best protection, of course, is a flaming valiant heart. A call for assistance may sometimes be necessary, better is to courageously repel the unwanted entities one's self but in the name and power of the Teacher. The sacred mantra, Om Ah Hum Vajra Guru Padma Siddhi Hum was give long ago to invoke the essential nature (*vajra*) and power (*siddhi*) of Teacher (*guru*) in the lotus (*padma*) of the heart (*hum*). Om, Ah, Hum are the seed syllables for the Three Principles, pure spirit, creative mind (psychic energy), and the heart essence. Some of the Knights of the Sacred Fire were followers of the Precious Teacher (Guru Rinpoche)[2] in former lives.

The Way of the Sacred Fire is marked by a refinement of consciousness in the unifying fire of the heart, the fire of spiritual sensitivity. When the Teacher says to **guard the treasure of the heart**, it means to conserve and maintain with vigilance this most precious energy. **Only the thread of the heart can lead to the Infinite.**[3]

The term heart, as it is used in the Teaching, has a broader meaning than is usually considered. It relates to a highly refined sensitivity of feeling, the source of which cannot be ascribed to oneself. **How necessary it is to feel one's heart, not as one's own, but as the universal One. It is beautiful to sense the heart as the sun of suns of the universe.** It is through this primordial heart essence that the yogi perceives higher truth. **To behold with the eyes of the heart, to listen with the ears of the heart to the roar of the world, to peer into the future with the comprehension of the heart, to remember the accumulations of the past through the heart. Thus must one impetuously advance upon the path of ascent.**[4]

---

[1] *Agni Yoga* 121 also see *Agni Yoga* 121, 122, & 127.
[2] Padmasambhava.
[3] *Hierarchy* 449
[4] *Heart* 1

29

The illumination of the consciousness is an experience of the heart. The heart unites the yogi with Infinity. The exaltation that the yogi experiences is due entirely to the illuminating fire of the heart, the fire of the enlightened consciousness. It is the responsibility of the yogi to maintain this exalted consciousness continuously.

The fire of the heart kindles surrounding fires creating a magnetic attraction. This act of service, which contains no imposition of will, awakens in others who seek it a powerful attraction to the Seed of Spirit. **The perception of the divine Fire in the Seed of the Spirit is the foundation for a new humanity.**[1]

Perception through the heart bestows a charm, which cannot be acquired with gold. The manifestation of Anura—in other words, charm of the heart—is very highly valued. It belongs to among the cumulative and indefinable qualities.[2]

The heart that has consecrated itself to righteousness radiates benevolence continuously, independently of the volitional sendings. Similarly, the sun's rays are not sent with premeditation.... The heart of goodness sows about itself health, smiles, and spiritual bliss....[3] It is necessary to visualize clearly the constant radiation of the heart.[4] This is one of the yogi's primary acts of service. **Do not tire of repeating about the necessity of realizing the application of the heart for the attracting of the highest possibilities.**

Throughout the Agni Yoga Books the Teacher has affirmed the creativeness of thought, that we are responsible for the quality of our thinking. **Consider thought as a creator.**[5] Thoughts continue to live on in space, even when our attention is turned elsewhere. Its creative power continues to affect the world for good or ill. **Benefit or harm it is you, the people, who predetermine. As the sending, so is the receiving. One may create a shower of radiant sendings, but one may also fill the space with locusts. Such is the**

---

[1] *Fiery World* III 253
[2] *Heart* 489
[3] *Heart* 63
[4] *Heart* 64
[5] *Infinity* I, 3

law of cooperation between thoughts and space. This is the basis for the benevolent law of karma, which will, if we pay attention to it, will bestow in us a sense of responsibility.

Man should free himself, the sooner the better, from the absurd ideas about the accidental nature of events. There is a cause for everything and it is wise to find its source. The hidden cause of events is the creative power of thought—psychic energy. This is the secret of karma.

From thought is born a physical action. So does the saturation of karma finally produce physical consequences.[1]

Karma is the effect of thought. Like attracts like. Through the Law of Attraction we draw to us like a magnet what ever we think about. Thus we can use the psychic energy, creative power of thought, to manifest what ever is needed for the greater good, or through negative thinking we will draw to us corresponding negative events. If our thoughts center around the strong and clear intension to unite with the Divine then we attract to us the necessary spiritual energies and events that will be needed to establish that union. If our intension is to harm we draw to ourselves harmful energies.

Since every thought is a magnet, each striving quest is a powerful magnet. These magnetic fluids are stratified in space forming the manifestation of magnetic poles. Striving creates a magnetic link between where you are now and the goal of your striving. This magnetic link acts as a conduit along which we journey to reach our wondrous future.

Verily, magnetization of the spirit can create powerful strata that will attract all of the great energies.[2] When we read and contemplate the Teaching we are, consciously or unconsciously, saturating space with powerful affirmations of truth. These affirmations are added to the kindred good thoughts and striving hearts of other students of the fiery Path, creating thereby powerful living thought-forms in step with the future destiny of the world. **The confirmation of the yogi of his path will be the full participation in the evolution of the world.**

Do not underestimate the powerful effect that a daily reading of the Teaching will have on those unknown kindred spirits with an affinity of

---

[1] *Fiery World* I, 625.
[2] *Fiery World* III, 205

auras. **We regard as an attainment not only the direct transmission of the Teaching, but also the indirect saturation of space with it.**[1]

Remember that the power of thought is many times stronger and ultimately more effective than physical actions! Materialists' will deny this, of course, but for them even consciousness is something physical. Thoughts that contain higher truths will inspire those who are seeking them. And when consciously generated with feelings of the heart they will more easily reach those who will utilize them for good. But in this we must be careful not to interfere with anyone's free will, particularly when sending thoughts to an individual. The Tibetan Buddhist practice of 'dedicating the merit,' is useful here; "May the fruit of my labor go for the liberation all sentient beings from suffering."

The saturation of space with formulas that clarify the Teaching will result in great effects. Thus do we affirm the New World. Thus is the manifestation of the predestined being brought about. This is particularly potent when accomplished as a group. **United sendings bring much usefulness when one tone can be maintained. One may even sound a leading note with a tuning fork.**[1]

The Agni Yoga Teaching is presented in essence and is usually not very specific. It therefore remains for the disciples to clothe the essential ideas into a form that can be better understood and utilized.

Everyone must think about the reconstruction of the world, for when we apprehend what is taking place, we grasp the approach of the future. Each thought directed to the construction of the New Epoch will produce its own forms. Thought-forms manifest the trend of the future; hence it is needful to understand the chain of saturated strivings. Creativeness of the spirit is as a fiery lever in space, as a powerfully impelled fiery creator, as a ruler in space, as a great saturating fire. Thus one who thinks about preeminence and about the great future molds an affirmation of constructiveness.

Space must be cemented with fiery formulas and fertilized by the manifest fire of the spirit. On the path to the Fiery World let us manifest striving for understanding of the reconstruction of the world.[1]

---

[1] *Fiery World* II, 181

Know how to direct your thought to the Common Good and we will always be with you.

The signs of Agni Yoga are many. **First will the inner fires of the centers be kindled. Then will ring out the voice of the unseen Teacher. And finally the external flame which seemingly binds the individual consciousness with the consciousness of space becomes manifest. Then will be possible the contact with the wondrous, perilous, subtlest energies, with all that which transforms life and invalidates the concept of death.**[2]

The voice of the unseen Teacher may resound to the inner ear like a clap of thunder. Perhaps only one word will be given, which when meditated upon will supply a wealth of useful information.

The term 'space' as use in the Teaching usually refers to spiritual space. **The Fire of Space**, for example, means the all-pervading Cosmic Fire. **The consciousness of space** means the all-encompassing, universal, primordial awareness.

You will behold the stars of the spirit; you will see the flames of purification of your centers; you will hear the voice of the Invisible Teacher; and you will acquire those subtlest perceptions that transform life.[3] With the kindling of the centers and the absorption of the Sacred Fire the yogi will occasionally experience the explosion of little colored sparks, which will unexpectedly flash before the vision. These 'sparks of Fohat,' which seem to be mostly blue or white, are an indication that the Sacred Fire is beginning to saturate the centers. They can also be sent by the Teacher to indicate danger, as encouragement, or as a confirmation of a realized truth. **I advise noting what actions and thoughts are accompanied by the appearances of the stars, and their colors and dimensions... One should simply observe to what thought they relate.**[4] **Pure striving produces flashes of fire. One has to observe these beginnings and the conditions that accompany them. For this purpose a true ability to observe keenly should be developed.**[5]

[1] *Fiery World* III, 169
[2] *Agni Yoga* 181
[3] *Agni Yoga* 185
[4] *Agni Yoga* 466
[5] *Agni Yoga* 413

The Fire or Light of the Higher World is not an entirely unusual manifestation. Far oftener than it is thought do these sparks penetrate the earthly strata. Indeed, they are explained as electrical manifestations. Their substance does not differ essentially from that which it has been agreed to call electricity, but such sendings emanate from the thought energy of the Higher World. Not by accident do such fires and lights flash out; either encouragement or forewarning or confirmation resound in these sendings of Light.[1]

If a spark strikes from your manuscript lines that ought to be erased, and underlines with blue light that which should be accepted, it means you have found a powerful co-worker.[2]

When you are with us, surrounded by our blue sparks, all is attainable.[3]

Sleep or vigilance, labor or rest, motion or repose, all carry us equally toward the fulfillment of life's plan. "It is like fallen leaves," say the timid. "It is like seeds for the sowing," say the wise. "It is like arrows of light," say the daring.[4] The end is assured. But in terms of human suffering and the joy of creative fulfillment the evolution of consciousness and spirit is dependent upon human activity, which can either retard or hasten the Path.

One of the signs of Agni Yoga is the indescribable joy of the heart. It is our constant companion and guide. When our link with the Precious Guru is strong it will be a constant reminder of the beauty of the spiritual world. The joy of the heart will be the best indication of the rightness of each step forward. If we temporally loose our way it will recede into the background. As we grow in spirit, as we maintain our connection and cooperation with the Hierarchy, this joy becomes a subtle, very beautiful, enlightenment. **Joy is a special wisdom.** It is our responsibility to maintain this constant joy of the

---

[1] *AUM 84*
[2] *Agni Yoga 490*
[3] *Agni Yoga 469*
[4] *Agni Yoga 36*

34

heart as it effects the inner life of our surroundings in a positive, beautiful way.

The Teacher will sometimes communicate with us by sending joy. This touch, which will usually last but a few seconds, will often correspond with a pure or significant thought, a correct decision, or some selfless action on our part. This is one of the ways in which we are guided.

As reverence and love for the Teacher grows so does the sacred fire of the heart. As this psychic energy is intensified, and as our feelings and thoughts become more and more motivated by the unifying subtle energy of the heart, so too will this same joy be generated by us from within. Eventually these two activities, the joy sent by the Teacher and the joy generated from within, will overlap and become as one. By sending joy the Teacher is thus emphasizing the heart's natural joyous response to the internal Presence. In this way we begin to see that the guidance of the Teacher is a natural introduction to our own internal spiritual receptivity. The Teacher represents for us the spiritual potentialities latent within us until such time as we can manifest them ourselves. By sending joy He is giving us a taste of our true spiritual nature. This he does in concordance with our selfless striving. Love, joy and enlightenment are three ways of describing the one indescribable experience of the heart.

Essential is the joy of life. It is not only a healing remedy but also the best helper for communion with us. Where does this stimulating feeling, called the joy of life, arise? It does not come from wealth or self-satisfaction, but is often experienced amidst the most grievous difficulties and persecutions. In times of stress, joy is especially valuable and healing. We call it the joy of Be-ness, for it does not depend on personal circumstances, success, or profit. This joy has no earthly reasons; it comes as a forerunner of the highest currents, which spiritualize the entire surrounding atmosphere.

Can there be feelings of joy when one is afflicted with disease or when one is the victim of injustice and insult? Indeed, for even in such circumstances the eyes may sometimes fill with fire, the bowed head may rise, and new strength may be experienced. Then one will begin to rejoice at life, perhaps not at one's own life, but at real Be-ness.

What strong thoughts will come to those who perceive the joy of Be-ness! The atmosphere around them will be purified, those near them will feel relief, and we will smile from afar and approve the better currents. We shall even be grateful, for each preservation of energy is benevolent.

Everyone who wants to succeed should remember the joy of life. Each person who wants to contact the better currents should know the path that will bring him to us. One need not fabricate special scientific reasons for such joy; it comes through the heart, and is absolutely real. This joy will enable one to better hear our calls.[1]

One of the signs of achievement is the discovery that certain states of consciousness can be generated spontaneously and held for as long as needed. These states of spiritual receptivity have their own flavor, so to speak, a definite exalted feeling that always accompanies successful contemplation along spiritual lines. We can therefore learn to bring these feelings forward as needed. States of a refined feeling nature can be invoked, such as solemnity, communion, calmness, generosity, patience, devotion, gratitude and the rest. **Any feeling can be cultivated.**[2]

Skills are the best discipline for the development of **patience and are within the reach of all.**[3] Skill takes will, persistence, and patience; skill in meditation, skill in a craft (in the creation of beauty), skill in the discipline of the Path. Will in needed to stay with it until perfected is reached. **Patience gives accuracy to our work and in the high quality of labor we shall understand the meaning of harmony.**

*A*ccording to the prophecy of the most ancient Teachers, when **humanity loses the foundation of the Teaching and sinks into obscurity, the Epoch of Maitreya will take plane.**[4] **Agni Yoga is being manifested as a forerunner of the Great Epoch—yes, yes, yes!**[5] One of the primary keynotes for the New Era is Fire—spiritual energy. The Egyptian Hieroglyph for

---

[1] *Supermundane* 281
[2] *Aum 93*
[3] *Supermundane 411*
[4] *Hierarchy 1*
[5] *Fiery World* III 168.

36

energy is also the sign for Aquarius. The key-note for the time of Aquarius is energy. Thus, the study and application of subtle energy in its dual capacity—radiant energy (magnetic) and force or directed energy (electric)—is so important at this time. Other keynotes of the Epoch of Aquarius also include Synthesis, Hierarchy, Beauty, Community, Women, Straight Knowledge, and Great Service.

At the beginning of the new epoch of Aquarius it is useful to view everything in terms of energy. This is particularly true when working with emotions, where it is essential to keep a detached perspective. Our lives are a complex composite of energies. Our thoughts and feelings are subtle energies, each with their own rate and quality of vibrations. Our purpose, as yogis, is to refine and transmute these subtle energies to the point where they vibrate in harmony with the impulse and direction of evolution. If we can do this we will soon discover that its all one energy, vibrating at different degrees of intensity and subtlety. **In life we can refine the keenness of our understanding of subtle energies, for in them is the future.**

One may compare Agni Yoga with the Morning Star, which heralds the approach of Light.[1] Agni Yoga directs our steps from the old world to the new, from Kali Yuga, the Age of Darkness, to Satya Yuga, the Age of Light. It marks the beginning of a great new direction in the spiritual evolution of humanity, **a great reorganization of the world**. At the beginning of Satya Yuga our **entire life must be adjusted for the new direction of evolution.**[2]

Like an inevitable cataclysm that seeps away whole continents, unavoidable is the Yoga of the Realization of Fiery Power.[3] The fire necessarily consumes the dross of the old world so that a New World can arise from the ashes.

We shall not tire of reminding you that one of the signs of Armageddon is the enormous increase in the numbers of false preachers. They appear in all countries and offer whatever the crowds desire.[4] They are

---

[1] *Agni Yoga* 179.
[2] *Agni Yoga* 173
[3] *Agni Yoga* 188
[4] *Supermundane* II 336

found in the marketplace selling their instructions and miraculous remedies for a profit. They can also be found disguised as angels of light, dictating half-truths with false conclusions, through gullible mediums.

The present time is severe. One can read in various Puranas about dates. If some scientists can calculate eclipses and earthquakes, other scientists can calculate other dates—the transition from the Kali Yuga to the Satya Yuga has been described with considerable accuracy, and the gravity of the time has been indicated.[1] According to the *Vishnu Purana* at the end of the Kali Yuga, "wealth will be decreasing day by day until nearly the whole world will be deprived. Property alone will confer rank. Devotion will be given to wealth alone. Passion will be the sole bond between the sexes. False-hood will be the only successful means of litigation. Women will be merely objects of sensual gratification. The Earth will be venerated only for its mineral treasures."

Armageddon was predicted ages ago, and the abnormalities at the end of Kali Yuga were described in the Puranas, but even keen thinkers underestimated those clear indications.[2] Armageddon, which is now upon us, is due to resistance, either consciously or unconsciously, to the fast approaching Satya Yuga, the Age of Light.

One may ask oneself, is not involution taking place? The end of the Kali Yuga can also produce such manifestations. Terrible cataclysms have been indicated, but what can be more frightful than a catastrophe of the spirit. No earthquake can be compared with the dissolution of consciousness. All forces need to be intensified in order to hold back humanity from the abyss, therefore meditation about the Higher World is a necessity of the day.[3] Prophecies concerning the number of deaths that will take place during his time often refer to spiritual deaths.

The time of Kali Yuga has been difficult, but Satya Yuga must again bring closer the worlds, which were forcibly separated. One must await this time solemnly as the return to a predestined perfection.[4] The Kali Yuga is the last of the four Yugas. This means that the beginning of Satya Yuga, the

---

[1] *Fiery World* 1: 395
[2] *Supermundane I*, 106 Also see *Bhagavata Purana* 12, chapter 2.
[3] *Aum* 236
[4] *Heart* 78

Age of Truth, is the beginning of a whole new cycle of Yugas. When the predestined New World is affirmed in the Teaching it should be taken literally, physically and spiritually. "And behold, new Heaven, and a new Earth," says St. John.

The New World cannot be built upon an old foundation; new wine cannot be stored in old containers. The transition from the old world to the new, therefore, must be a time of fiery purification. **Indeed the atmosphere surrounding the planet is saturated with wails of imperfection. And the auras of mankind are so physically and spiritually infected that only a fiery cleansing can give salvation. Halfway measures bring no purification; therefore one must become accustomed to the thought of a powerful cleansing, for the firmament is in need of severe measures. Thus, humanity must atone for all its creations and all outrages that have taken root so deeply in the consciousness.**[1]

Each Epoch leaves its impress in Eternity. Thus Babylon fell, thus Rome fell, thus the sands have covered civilizations, and waters engulfed empires. But for the change of our cycle there approaches the most fiery, and the greatest, destruction and construction. Space is saturated with fiery energies for reorganization. Extraordinary is the time; the fire is raging![2]

The appointed hour is approaching and people will either understand what is predestined or choose catastrophe. The torrents of blood cannot be washed away. But new scourges will purge the earth of its evil.[3] **The stage that the planet is going through can be compared with the furnace of cosmic fire. All dense energies are aflame in tension, and on guard stands the Fiery Right**, the Hierarchy. **Fiery creativeness is assembling all fiery energies—thus the world is being reconstructed by the tension of the two polarities**, the old world and the new. **It is necessary to discern these turbulent energies.**

At the beginning of each new epoch new energies enter into life to establish the quality and direction of the spiritual evolution of the period. These descending energies, these **currents of evolution** or **rays** as they are

---

[1] *Fiery World* III, 177
[2] *Fiery World* III, 175
[3] *Leaves of M's Garden* N.Y. June 9 1921

39

called in the Teaching, give the **fiery impulse** for humanities next step forward. But because the psychic pollution that surrounds and permeates the consciousness of this world is so dense these new energies cannot manifest purely without fiery purification.

Purification of the foundations must be affirmed, for without this it is impossible to manifest the New World. The degeneration of the foundations is ruinous; and pure energies cannot be attracted to the earthly plane without transmutation of the accumulations that are stifling the planet. How then to affirm the New World? As has been said—with fire and sword! Yes, Yes, Yes!

Verily a New World! The joy of the spirit provides all possibilities. When the great future is affirmed, our creativity embraces all manifestations. When we are assembling a New Race, we intensify all achievements.[1]

1. The core of the planet is surround by energies that infuse life into all its processes. But in tensity the planet has varied from its original saturation. Indeed, it cannot be denied that the two poles are out of balance. The counter-position is a result of their having one and the same source. Each encirclement of the planet brings an accumulation of energy.

The 'core' (the essential nature) of the planet is surrounded by those divine energies that infuse (saturate) life and purpose into the evolutionary processes. However, due to the intensity of the free will energies of its human inhabitants, the intended absorption of these divine energies has been blocked. Indeed, it cannot be denied that the two poles, human free will and the current of evolution, are out of balance; they are not in cooperation. The counter-position in the world arena of these poles is due to there having one and the same source. Each encirclement of the planet, each new cycle, brings a new accumulation (saturation) of the divine evolutionary energy.

Two energies are being discussed here. The divine **current of evolution**, which **infuses new life and purpose into the evolutionary process**, and the often opposing energies produced by the free will activity of humanity. At our present point in evolution, these two poles are not in balance. This is the root cause of humanities difficulties.

---

[1] *Infinity* II, 110

2. The currents of evolution are transforming the Earth and generating a new step in its evolution. However, the manifestation of a predestined date for this new step evokes all alternate and opposing currents. In other words, opposing forces step in to stop the manifestation of the new energies. All dormant energies, the good as well as the evil, are aroused and all that is subject to destruction is strained. Shall the heart not quiver when the flame of conflagration and destruction engulfs all spheres? All the departing and all self-asserting energies, all that is of the old world and are therefore moving contrary to the flow of evolution are determining their tension of will in opposition. This is the great battle spoken of throughout the Teaching. The East awakens and opposes the West; the North opposes the South—and shall the heart not quiver? Ominous are the currents. The purified spirit assimilates (is receptive to) all of their courses, all the lines of force of the evolutionary currents. The cosmic verdict for the planet is austere but full of limitless beauty. As we (the Hierarchy) in the Tower follow the gathering of the new threads of evolution, so you also must perceive all the movements of the currents of the element of Fire.

Verily, the centers of an Agni Yogi feel each planetary vibration. Hence, it is so imperative to strive toward us, toward the Hierarchy, during these cosmic perturbations. Just as we share in the destiny of the planet, so we also partake of the beauty of the Infinite.

3. The aura of man, which is affirmed for the reception of the cosmic transmission of divine energies, just as does any conductor of electricity. When the human spheres require certain shocks, the cosmic transmissions flow accordingly. Only those elements, only those spiritual energies, adhere to, or remain in, the human spheres and can be absorbed by the affirmed auras. When spheres require violent destruction it means that those spheres cannot absorb the streaming transmissions of Cosmos. Hence, the darkness surrounding the planet will never permit the affirmation of the cosmic Fire without the manifestation of explosions. These forces of purification will illumine humanity. The cosmic fires attract the affirmed dates. The 'affirmed' is that which is destined.

New spiritual energies are streaming into our world from cosmic sources. Due to the darkness of the times, and a resistance of free will, these

41

evolutionary currents are not being adequately absorbed by humanity, thus causing explosions. And while these explosions may be catastrophic in nature they will eventually purify and illuminate humanity.

4. **The purifying fires of the Universe penetrate all regions of the planet. The sparks of conflagration** and destruction **spread along all channels** according to karma. **As volcanoes, these affirmed fires explode. The force of karma shifts and transfers power from hand to hand,** from nation to nation. The cosmic course of evolution **is directed toward those purifying conflagrations; hence the comet, speeding through the Infinite. The** intensity **of the currents is very great and the effect** of these evolutionary currents **corresponds to the fires of the planet. The centers of the Agni Yogi record all cosmic currents.**

5. **The magnetic currents of the human aura penetrate the densest regions. Certainly, science must call these emanations psychic energy. Indeed, adjustments should be made** by humanity **in regard to these manifestations of inexhaustible energy,** so that they will more readily correspond to the spiritual currents. **The intensive properties of the will** can **propel the psychic seeds** into space to **form a sphere conducive to** spiritual **striving.** Psychic seeds are creative living thought-forms that can be created by humanity to either further the spiritual evolution of the world or as acts of destruction. **The nature of these emanations** of psychic energy **can produce a powerful tension** in the world. **Depending upon the way the streams of these emanations of a blended aura** of humanity **are directed, the power of this energy is either destructive or constructive. Thus, from human emanations it will be possible to derive the most diverse energies. Conscious handling of the emanations of the human aura will afford an achievement of great fiery creativeness.** The Knights of the Sacred Fire consciously utilize the creative power of psychic energy to saturate space, from their blended aura, psychic seeds in concordance with evolution.

6. **The irradiation** of the psychic energy **of the human aura can intensify a powerful energy** in the object, body, or person. **The propelled stream** of the subtle energy **of a center can melt** (transmute) **an intensified energy** in body one wishes to transmute. Transmutation occurs when the core of the object, or body is stimulated (intensified) through the action of psychic

42

energy. **Hence, when streams of blue fire pour from the fingers, it is the creativeness of the emanations** of psychic energy **that manifests the action of** transmutation. **Thus do the centers create. The spiritual transmissions are intensified by the same energies. All creative processes are thus strained** (intensified) **by the centers. The process of creativeness of the centers is so subtle that it is invisible. Of course the centers act creatively on many planes.** The astral and mental bodies also have centers that create using subtle energies. **The creativeness of the propelled irradiation** of the centers even **strives** (wills itself) **into the spheres of the far-off worlds. Creative emanations** of the centers can **truly magnetize space**. This is the primary mission of all true Agni Yogis.

Let our words about Fire not be regarded as abstract symbols. I speak of Fire truly existing. This is not the first time that the planet will experience the effect of this element. During each change of race Fire approaches as a purifying stream. Humanity remembers the devastation caused by the fusion of the Fire of Space with its subterranean fiery precipitates. Why repeat the destruction of Atlantis if it is possible to attract the beneficial aspects of the element of fire? [1]

St. John, in his *Book of Revelation,* predicted that during Armageddon one of the scourges visited upon humanity as a result of their karma was a fiery epidemic. **Remember that this epidemic was foreseen long ago. When we spoke about Armageddon, we had in mind not only war, but all the devastating consequences of humanity's confusion. But one should not fall into despair, for a depressed state opens the door to all that is poisonous. It is wise to know that Armageddon is accompanied by epidemics.** [2]

The Teaching of evolution shows that human timidity increases before the change of race. But the date approaches, and those who have not learned to swim must swallow their fill of the brine. [3]

The violence of this destruction is determined by the amount of resistance generated by humanity against this new direction of evolution.

---

[1] *Agni Yoga* 341
[2] *Supermundane 435*
[3] Agni Yoga 47

Although we shall not weary of reiterating about magnanimity, yet this is the last chance for many to realize it. Pay attention to the word LAST.[1]

The situation in the world is difficult; everywhere there is a kind of ossification. People think to entrench themselves in a bog, but whole mountains are splitting as a reminder of what is coming[2]

The New World cannot be built upon an old foundation. It is therefore natural that before each new epoch, before each new redirection of the currents of evolution, the remnant of the old cycle must pass away. **Thus Babylon fell, thus Rome fell, thus the sands have covered civilizations, and waters engulfed empires. But as to the coming change of our cycle there approaches the fieriest and the greatest of all destructions and constructions. The coming New Cycle will be a major rather than a minor change. Space is saturated with fiery energies for the reorganization. Extraordinary is the time; the Fire is raging![3]**

The purpose of divine destruction, which always precedes the beginning of a great new cycle, besides clearing the field for a new construction, involves a purification of the organisms so that they may more easily assimilate the new energies. In the Teaching this is called 'fiery purification,' and 'the purification of space.'

The dates are approaching. Displacement of the old world for the new is being affirmed in the very depths of the planet, in the very depths of nations, in the very depths of life. The cycle affirms displacement of the old cycle and the arrival of new principles. Thus do we create together the New World.[4]

On the path to the fiery world let us remember the law of fiery purification.[5]

A great reorganization is coming! The scales are now being tipped. New evolutionary currents are descending upon us bringing new impulses to unify and progress along new lines. This reorganization of the patterns

---

[1] *Fiery World* I, 121
[2] *Fiery World* I, 125
[3] *Fiery World* III, 175
[4] *Fiery World III*, 232
[5] Fiery World III, 177

and energies of the way forward, though necessary for a truer alignment with evolution, is bringing to the surface the results of humanity's karma.

In cosmos there is a most gigantic equilibrium. It is this cosmic equilibrium that is the force and measure behind the manifestation of accumulated karma. **The power of the equilibrium is maintained through a harmonized psycho-life.** The psychic life of humanity adds, for good or ill, its energies to the cosmic creation. **The more errors on the one hand, the more enlightenment on the other** to offset it and preserve the balance. **The striving of the awakened spirits increases in proportion with the decline of the general trend of thought. Great is the Law of Equilibrium!** [1]

$\mathcal{Y}$oga is the path to spiritual unity through self-mastery. Hatha Yoga pertains to the mastery of the body. Bhakti Yoga pertains to the mastery of the emotional nature. Karma Yoga pertains to the mastery of one's time and activity. Raja Yoga pertains to the mastery of the mind. Agni Yoga pertains to the mastery of one's fire, one's psychic energy. Agni Yoga, the Way of the Sacred Fire, includes the earlier given yogas. Bhakti Yoga or union with the divine through love and devotion, transmutes negative emotions and attachments into wisdom and love. **Fly by love and you will realize the joy of flying.**[2] One of the fundamental principles of Agni Yoga is the truth that wisdom arises not through the rational mind, but rather through the essential nature of the heart. **To see with the eyes of the heart,** is enlightenment divine. Agni Yoga also includes Raja Yoga, which leads to spiritual union through mastering the activity of the mind. **Therefore, hail we the most ancient—Raja Yoga, and affirm we the future—Agni Yoga.**

Yoga—as that supreme span, or connecting link, **with all cosmic attainments —has existed through all ages. Each Teaching comprises its own Yoga, applicable to that step of evolution. Yogas do not contradict each other. As branches of one tree they spread their shade and refresh the traveler exhausted from heat. His strength regained, the traveler continues on his way. He accepts naught that was not his; nor does he divert his striving.** The Yogi realizes that he personally owns nothing in the material

---

[1] *Infinity* 1, 91
[2] *Leaves of Morya's Garden 1, 328*

world and that his only true possessions are those that he can take with him from life to life, his attainments. **He embraces the manifested Benevolence of Space** (represented by the Hierarchy). **He liberates the preordained forces** (within himself). **And he masters his single belonging,** (his consciousness). **Do not reject the forces of Yoga, but as light let them search the twilight of labor unrealized.** The forces of yoga, which are the forces of spiritual evolution itself, will reveal to us those areas of imperfection in ourselves where labor is needed. **For the future, we arise out of sleep. For the future we renew our garments,** transforming them into bodies of light. **For the future we sustain ourselves, for the future we strive in our thoughts**. **For the future we gather strength. First shall we apply the counsels of life. Then shall we pronounce the name of the Yoga of the time approaching** –the yoga of Agni, the Sacred Fire. **We shall hear the tread of the element of Fire, but we shall already be prepared to master the undulations of the flame.**[1]

Agni Yoga embraces many of the primary principles of Mahayana Buddhism as (1) the altruistic motivation to follow the spiritual path for sake of all beings, (2) the emphasis upon the realization of selflessness and sacrifice for the sake of others, (3) in its reverence and devotion to the guiding Community of Bodhisattvas *(Sangha)*, (4) the affirmation of the foundation, pure Be-ness *(tathata)*, and (5) in the realization of universal synthesis *(sunyata)*.

The prayer of the Fiery Knights is always: **May my path be marked with the attainment of selflessness.**[2] Selflessness is the realization that in the essence we are not separate beings, but rather we are one with all life, with all beings. In this achievement the individual ego disappears. The realization of selflessness is true identification with life itself. The personal will never enter the Kingdom of Heaven. But the personal can be transformed into the divine.

People may ask which yoga is the shortest path to knowledge. You know of Agni Yoga—the fiery synthesis—but many have not yet familiarized themselves with this fiery knowledge. They would like to be directed to one of the earlier known yogas. I shall select the Karma Yoga,

---

[1] *Agni Yoga* Preface.
[2] *Fiery World* 7

46

which includes creativeness, conscious labor, striving towards higher quality. It will lead to the Highest by the shortest path. However, Karma Yoga requires time, whereas Agni Yoga can be called the lightning-like way. Think how beautiful is the path of lightning, but do not forget how difficult the lightning-like tension is.[1]

This most synthesizing yoga extracts an obligation to construct one's entire life in accordance with a discipline that is externally imperceptible. The yogi displays no outward signs of distinction, no priestly robes or display of austerity. The self-imposed disciplines of the yogi are internal. If we sense the presence of an Agni Yogi it will be due to his or her inner heart magnetism.

If the essential discipline is not seen as chains but is perceived as the joy of responsibility, we can consider the first gates open. When cooperation with the far-off worlds is embraced, then will the second gates be unbarred. Cooperation with the spiritual world, with Hierarchy, means to align one's forces behind the evolution of the world. And when the foundations of evolution are understood, the bolts will fall from the third gates. Evolution is the natural unfolding of the spiritual destiny of the world, directed from the Higher Worlds in such a way that it does not interfere with the freewill of humanity. And finally, when the superiority of the densified astral body has been recognized then will the locks of the fourth gates fall away.[2] The densified astral sheath is created so that the yogi can more easily appear to those in need wherever they are in the world.

You who strive to enter the ranks of the Knights of the Sacred Fire, be forewarned! This path is not easy. It leads to the joy of spiritual freedom, creative power, and an illuminated consciousness. It also leads to labor and sacrifice for the sake of the world! It leads to Kurukshetra, the spiritual battleground! The Fiery Knights drink the poison of the world, transforming it into Amrita, the elixir of immortality.

For the performance of a superb musical creation one chooses perfectly tuned instruments. When such instruments are few the pressure of

---

[1] *Supermundane* Book 4, 767
[2] *Agni Yoga* 163

47

the currents fall upon the few.[1] Though few in number the Fiery Knights fearlessly bare the burden of the world. Difficult unless the heart is open and the will is strong. It must not be thought that we are traveling on a luxury train—we are walking over an abyss on a plank.[2] Whoever is sure in his will—let him enter![3]

It is essential to not mislead newcomers into thinking the Teaching of Agni Yoga is easy. It is not easy, for there is much tension and danger in it. No one should be seduced by the idea of honeyed ease. Gaining mastery of the fires is a slow process.[4] We purposely emphasize the difficult side; first, in order not to hide the truth, and second, if man realizes the joy of spiritual achievement, he will also realize that even the greatest difficulties are nothing when compared with the grandeur of illumination.[5]

The first calls are pleasant and benevolent and the status of the guarded ward is not a responsible one. But as the consciousness grows the spirit becomes worthy of special missions. And because each mission is antagonistic to the old mundane logic it is therefore subject to difficulties and dangers. Verily, there are few who learn to rejoice at the conquest of obstacles. Many are even ready to regret the loss of their bygone average consciousness. The commands of the Teacher become brief. Therefore, the work depends to a large degree on independent action. Friends become rare, obstructions are piled up like unapproachable mountains, and victories are apparently indiscernible. Even the effects of the subtlest energies are not readily apparent.... But above all rises the fulfillment of the desire to further the general good. Spiritual cooperation grows, unlimited by space. Through the manifesting substance of the far-off worlds the relationship to one's surroundings changes and the spatial work of creating beneficial thought-forms for the common good ceases to be an empty sound. The assigned missions become a joy, as if they were one's own inalienable labor. It cannot be otherwise. Of course this joy is not in the gambols of a goat. The evaluation of the surroundings makes stern the

---

[1] *Agni Yoga* 306.
[2] *Community* 76
[3] *Agni Yoga* 222
[4] *Agni Yoga* 403
[5] *Supermundane* 132

faces of the workers, but life is transformed and from the heights one observes the coils of the earthly dragon. Fearlessness, already transmitted in the first call, brings one closer to the new waves of light, the new possibilities destined for humanity.[1]

One of the primary techniques of the Fiery Yoga is Tactica Adversa, using adversity as an aid to the path. I rejoice if you understand that obstacles are really opportunities.[2] But for this we must take action, we must enter the battle. Battle is our destiny, and one must include it in the daily plan.[3] When your step is firm, the counterforces are beneficial. The future is constructed by lightning-bolts of realization. The power of these great sparks depends upon the strength of the counterforce. Clearly then, success will not come form embarking on a voyage in a tub across a stagnant pool. When we say, 'set sail,' we mean that you must try the ocean; the grandeur of its waves will give you joy. Does not the testing of one's strength lead to a growth of power?[4]

Let no one be disconcerted by my demand for battle. Those who stand on one spot are a thousand times more exposed to danger than those who strive. However, the striving must be in the heart and thoughts, and not only in the feet.[5] We are often accused of frightening people by putting so much stress on the concept of battle and for saying that our battle is endless. People assume that creation is peaceful, and battle destructive, but how can one think of creation without mastery over the elements, without a courageous struggle to overcome obstacles?[6]

The Great Pilgrim (the Christ) was frequently attacked by the forces of darkness. These incidents were mentioned in the Scriptures, and one might question how occurrences that no one had witnessed could have been recorded. It was the Teacher Himself who wanted to prepare His disciples for that battle and therefore, rather than conceal the struggle that was taking place, He recounted His own experiences to illustrate it. He

---

[1] *Agni Yoga* 273
[2] *Agni Yoga* 494
[3] *Agni Yoga* 179
[4] *Agni Yoga 257*
[5] *Fiery World* I 36
[6] *Supermundane* 78

said, "Every human being constantly finds himself in three battles. Although he may imagine that he is completely at peace, he actually takes part in three battles simultaneously.[1]

The first battle is between the free will and karma. Nothing can excuse man from taking part in the struggle between these two principles— to align one's free will with the flow of spiritual evolution. When this is accomplished no karma is accumulated. The second battle takes place between the disembodied entities of good and evil, which surround man and influence him in one way or another. These entities may remain hidden so that their whisperings are taken for one's one thoughts, or they might pretend to be guides or angles of light or there maybe disruptions at night during sleep. The Master protects the students until such time as they can begin to protect themselves.

The third battle resounds in the Infinite, in space, between the subtle energies of order and the waves of chaos. The human imagination is too limited to envision these battles in Infinity.[2]

The preceding yogas, given from the highest sources, took as their basis a particular aspect of life. Now, at the dawn of the Age of Maitreya, there is needed a yoga comprising the essence of the whole of life, all-embracing, evading naught. One remembers the example of those unignitable youths in the biblical legend who valiantly sacrificed themselves to the fiery furnace and thereby acquired power… It is precisely the element of fire that gives its name to this yoga of self-sacrifice.[3]

When a hero dedicates himself to the salvation of mankind he multiplies his strength tenfold.[4]

By divine right do we forge the Sword of Spirit. By divine right do we enter the Sangha of Maitreya. With a pure heart do we affirm the path of power for the sake of the world! The Yogi of the Sacred Fire is not an instrument nor passive recipient, but a co-worker and creator. He walks like a lion.[5]

---

[1] *Supermundane* 161
[2] *Supermundane* 161
[3] *Agni Yoga* 158
[4] *Fiery World* 150
[5] *Agni Yoga* 225

As we will be passing through uncharted territory, and dealing with unknown and often hostile forces, the guidance and protection of our wise and powerful Friend will be an absolute necessity. He will protect us from those forces that we cannot yet handle alone. But we must be sure of our path and our Guide before beginning, for once we have accepted Him, and He has accepted us, it is unfitting, even dangerous, to change our mind half way up the mountain. If this sounds like a threat then this path is not for you. Is it really a threat to warn someone of the dangers that lie ahead? If we sever the lifeline connecting us with the lead climber half way up the mountain the danger of falling becomes a real possibility. To blame our Guide for our own missteps will cause us to loose our way. Our Captain will not abandon us, but we must be very careful not to abandon him, even with a thought. **How the heart must be guarded lest it sever the silver cord!** [1]

At a certain stage on the path the protection of a radiant shield becomes necessary.[2] **A protective net must surround the body…Teros** (heart energy) **and Tamas** (vital energy or prana) **must work together like brothers. The outward radiance of heart energy is combined with a strengthening of the vitality of the aura. The strengthening of the aura occurs through communion with the higher world, as egotism falls away and selflessness is kindled. It is the spirit that imbues the aura with radiation, but the protective network makes it compact. It encloses it and helps it to keep the energy from dissipating. By the realization of the defensive net one can protect the radiations from dissipating; but it is impossible to stretch** (extend) **the network without Teros, the ray of which, like a lantern, must find and fill the vital breaks in the aura.** With the defense net in place we are protected from the conditioning currents of the mass mind, making it easier to hear and feel the inner rhythms of the divine. **At first glance the leaping sparks seem to be only the motion of the apparatus; but they are guardians ready to repel the enemy.** [3]

---

[1] *Hierarchy* 275
[2] See *Leaves of Morya's Garden* Vol. II pages 90 & 91 #20 & p. 139-40 Also see *Fiery World* volume 2, 53
[3] *Leaves of Morya's Garden* 2, 168

Since ancient times, people have been advised at the hour of turmoil to repeat a short invocation and by rhythmic repetitions to repulse the wave of influences. Later, these measures deteriorated into the senseless repetition of religious words; nevertheless the principle remains sound . . . Of course, the power is not in the words themselves but in the creation of waves (rhythmic vibrations). The fact is that sometimes through the invocation of the spirit a useful wave (vibration) can be created. But habits are like numbness, under which even a powerful remedy ceases to act. When a poisonous breath is about to touch one, it is best to exhale. Likewise, one can create by will power a protecting veil.

The best armor is the fiery one. Can the leader proceed by the ordained path without the fiery armor? With what other means may one deflect all arrows of malice and swords of hatred? More than once have I spoken about the fire of the heart. Precisely this armor is a magnet, which attracts and protects. As it has been said, 'I will receive all arrows in my shield.' But the shield must be forged. This shield can be manifested only from above. But how many thoughts and discourses must be sent in advance, in order that this communion be established and the fiery armor be forged! One should lose not a day, nor an hour, to make the communion living and ever present.[1]

Among the fires of the heart the most vivid is the flame of self-sacrifice. Precisely this armor diverts the hostile arrows and creates the renowned invulnerability. The fire of courage is only a part of the flame of self-sacrifice. Of course, self-sacrifice does not necessarily mean to offer oneself as a victim, but rather it corresponds to the readiness to conquer for the work of the Highest World.[2]

The Knights of the Sacred Fire raise the banner of Maitreya, on which is depicted a cross and a chalice filled with the Sacred Fire. In Tibet images of Maitreya, the coming Buddha, all depict Him as holding a vase containing amrita, the elixir of Life ( ), to be poured out for the regeneration and

---

[1] *Fiery World* II 53
[2] *Heart* 536

transformation of the world. **Amrita consists of the accumulations of the finest energies.**[1] The Epoch of Maitreya is also known as the Age of Aquarius, the Water Bearer, with much the same symbolism. Aquarius is ruled by Mercury, ☿ which is also depicts the cross and the chalice. The chalice, at the crown, contains the Sacred Fire. The cross, at the heart, represents the dual life of the knight. Upward striving united with horizontal outreach in service to the world. The fiery knights no longer withdraws from life, but in cooperation with the Brotherhood, labors to bring into manifestation the destined New World. The Teacher relates a story of a disciple who says to his teacher; "In my exaltation I bumped my nose." It was pointed out to him that even in the exaltation of the path of ascent one must not loose one's equilibrium. The upward ascent must not interfere with one's labor for the sake of the world.

The Knights of the Sacred Fire have all dedicated their lives in service to the world. They are spiritual activists who labor to **link the earthly consciousness with the cosmic pulse.** They have united their hearts and minds with the Buddha Nature, the Christos, the Atma (call it what you will) within all beings. They are mastering their thoughts and feelings. They can live, with equal ease, in a hut or a palace. They do not consider themselves the owner of things, but rather their temporary guardian. They see difficulties as possibilities for growth. They know, in their heart of hearts, that behind it all is love. They radiate a spiritual magnetism that powerfully affects the lives of all they meet. The Knights of Fire understand that luxury, self-satisfaction, and an excess of physical comfort are deadly to the spiritual life. They choose to follow the impulse of the heart rather than desire. They understand that the heart contains both love and wisdom.

The Knights of the Sacred Fire will look for similarities in others before differences. They will discard all that leads to separation, all that is ugly, and all that is no longer useful. The fiery knights understand that the realization of selflessness and non-separation are fundamental to the path. They will give aid when needed, but they are careful not to give too much. The fiery Yogis will remain flexible and not become entangled. Their hearts are open to beauty and are therefore filled with joy. They understand the

---

[1] *Agni Yoga* 207

53

creative power of thought and are therefore vigilant, taking full responsibility for the quality of their thoughts, nipping in the bud thoughts that are unworthy.

The Knights of the Sacred Fire respond to fiery impulse of Evolution by making use of the creative power of thought, without interfering in the freewill of others. In this they practice harmlessness. They understand that the energy of thought attracts corresponding energies form space, which thereby stimulates the manifesting ideas. When the yogis contemplate a profound seed-thought of higher truth, for example, holding it at a point of tension, they draw to themselves like a magnet the realization of that truth. The illumination thus stimulates corresponding areas of the consciousness into greater activity, both in themselves and in others. The fiery yogis understand that it is important to distinguish between belief and direct perception.

The seed-thoughts given in the Agni Yoga Teaching contain living archetypal thought forms appropriate for our present stage in evolution. By meditating upon them we draw their essential nature into manifestation, thereby saturating space with meaning, for the benefit of the world. The Knights of the Sacred Fire utilize the creativeness of the power of thought to hasten the evolution of consciousness, that humanity may recover its lost estate.

$\mathcal{P}$roclaiming the new Era of Fire means that it is necessary to master this element. Fire and energy are synonymous terms. To master the fire means to master psychic energy. This is accomplished by mastering the mind and the subtle feeling nature. The sword of psychic energy is mastered by utilizing it in service to the world. It is strengthened by the spiritual tension created by overcoming the obstacles to the path. **The forging of the sword in the flame under the hammer's blow is the best illustration of how to temper one's psychic energy.**[1] The hammer's blow is opposition to the Way.

Psychic energy must not only be strengthened. It must also be refined.[2] The dictionary defines refinement as "the act of reducing to a pure

---

[1] *Agni Yoga* 602
[2] *Agni Yoga* 502

state through the elimination of all course characteristics." **The level of psychic energy can be determined according to its quality, not its power.**[1] Psychic energy is refined in the fire of the heart. When this is accomplished its natural state is perceived as beautiful and pure. Self-centered emotions and desires are thereby transmuted into wisdom and love. Eventually the refining of the psychic energy reaches a point where every nuance of spiritual sensitivity can be clearly distinguished. This is called the 'education of the heart.' Emotions arise in relation to oneself. Heart sensitivity arises in relation to others, in relation to the greater whole. The education of the heart learns to clearly distinguish between these two energies, the strictly personal and the universal.

The creative forces of thought can be mastered by applying the Teaching in life, by disciplining one's thoughts, and through one-pointed meditation. **The mastery of thought consists not only in the deepening and concentration of thinking;** but **one must also possess the knowledge of how to free oneself from untimely and debasing thoughts. Thus** the creative power of **thought is affirmed when we master it.**[2] The act of freeing oneself from unworthy thoughts must be continuous. **Even sleep vigilantly.**[3] To expel unwanted thoughts it is sometimes useful to immediately force them out with a strong expiration of the breath. **Notice that a deep sigh accompanies any application of psychic energy.**[4] This is a hint pertaining to the close connection that exists between the breath and the application psychic energy. This can be observed in the practice of pranayama. The outbreath facilitates the projection of psychic energy. The inbreath facilitates its intake.

Regard thought as a real force in life, then gain firm control over the flow of thought.[5] The field of battle is the sphere of thought. When we first attempt to control the flow of thoughts we discover that they are like undisciplined children thinking what ever they like. To gain firm control requires continuous effort. The fiery knights gain control of the mind by

---

[1] *Agni Yoga* 447
[2] *Fiery World* II, 227
[3] *Leaves of Morya's Garden* II, Preamble.
[4] *Agni Yoga* 603
[5] *Agni Yoga* 101

holding it at a high point of tension, calmly focused on the image of the Teacher. One of the primary purposes of meditation is to gain control of psychic energy.

The psychic activity of the mind, emotions, and heart sensitivity naturally produces corresponding activity of the energies of the nerve centers of the ethereal body. **Psychic energy like fire pervades all of space and condenses in the nerve centers.**[1] This is how the wondrous Philosopher's Stone is created. From this natural condensation process we can gain an understanding of how the natural creativeness of the psychic energy determines the health or lack of health of the body. **Various defects in the character are often reflected as physical flaws.**[2] **Spiritual health is the primary basis of bodily health.**[3] When the consciousness is refined the energies of the centers are refined as well. **The external conditions of life are a reflection of the consciousness.**[4] **People cannot conceive of ethics as being a practical pharmacopoeia for attracting spatial energies by the simplest method.**[5] A whole book could, and should, be written concerning this very basic and profound law of Nature. The laws of physics and the laws governing the activity of the human psyche are the same laws. The two worlds are not separate, but are interdependent and act together as a single unit. One of the problems with working with this truth, in healing for example, lies in the fact that due to the extreme density of the physical plane there is often a considerable lag time between psychic activity and the natural manifestation of its energy in the material world. **Joy can attract with a magnetic current the joy of space. But the thought of darkness gives birth to layers of heavy clouds.**

In Sanskrit the pure psychic energy of the heart is called *Ojas*, though this term has higher and lower corresponding meanings. In the same way that *Tejus*, the vital energy in food, and *Prana,* the vital energy in the air we breath, nourishes the body, so *Ojas*, the subtle energies of a refined feeling nature, nourishes and expands the consciousness. Both *Ojas* and *Prana* are

---

[1] *Heart* 506
[2] *Agni Yoga* 529
[3] *AUM 57*
[4] *Agni Yoga* 604
[5] *Heart* 104

subtly invoked from Space through the practice of yoga. The Gayatri Mantra, which is said to embody the essence of Vedas, invokes the Sacred Fire on three levels—prana from the ethereal sun, heart energy from the heart of the sun, and the Sacred Fire itself from the Spiritual Sun. It is useful to silently recite this mantra facing the morning sun with a flaming heart, keeping its meaning firmly in the consciousness.

It is a fundamental law of nature that whatever we think about is stimulated by our psychic energy. Attention is subtle energy and thought creates. Negative emotions, therefore, are best eliminated by starving them to death. If we do not feed them with the energy of our attention they will die from lack of nourishment. To master psychic energy means to gain control over where we place our attention. This may take years to master, but when accomplish we are liberated to a large extent from external conditioning. **It is not so difficult to transform and kindle the consciousness when constant attention is applied to it.**[1]

Self-mastery is our spiritual responsibility as its beneficial effects will strongly affect the world around us. **Attain and conquer. You do not conquer for yourself, but your victorious state is important for the general good**.

It is not easy to learn to think. It is difficult to develop intensity of thought, and even more difficult to attain thought of high quality.... It is necessary to exercise thought, not mentally but with the fire of the spirit, until all disunity of thought disappears. Thought can have power only if it is monolithic.... It is necessary to devote the needed time to the mastering of thought, but at the same time repeatedly remind yourself that all thought has one essence. The creative fire of thought is mastered not only through concentration but by the penetrating, as a point of spiritual tension, deep into the fiery essence of itself. **We rejoice at diversity of thinking, but each thought must be pure as a diamond.**[2]

Consider thought as a creator.[3] Thoughts saturate space, where they remain active, as a living energy, even when the attention is turned elsewhere. Good thoughts as well as dark thoughts have a powerful beneficial effect

---

[1] *Fiery World* I, 50
[2] *Agni Yoga* 345
[3] *Infinity* I: 3

57

upon one's surroundings. **Joy can attract with a magnetic current the joy of space. But the thought of darkness gives birth to layers of heavy clouds.**[1]

The mission of the sacred Order of Fiery Knights is, in part, the saturation of space with those timely truths so necessary for our transition from the old world to the new. These thoughts-forms become powerful impulses directing those that tune into them (usually unconsciously) to take steps in harmony with Evolution. This service takes place whenever we read and clearly contemplate the Teaching. If we can keep this in mind while reading the influence for good is greatly increased. In this way we give purpose to the living thought-forms. And if we add to this the fact that the ideas presented in the Teaching are being read by other strong-minded kindred spirits and are thus uniting in space we can begin to understand its creative power to lead us to the freedom of the higher worlds.

Can one ascend and descend in isolation? Truly, no being can act without affecting his surroundings. Not only does he stir up the various layers of the atmosphere with each action, but he literally drags his near ones with him. Man must realize his responsibility toward the universe. With each elevation of the spirit we are of substantial aid to others. But a person falling in spirit may thereby even kill someone. Beyond the range of one's conscious thought flows a constant unconscious interaction, embracing wide circles, limited by the law of karma and the affinity auras. We are responsible for the quality of our thoughts! Karma is the effect of the creativeness of thought. The psychic energy of those thoughts that are not is harmony with the Way remain in the person's atmosphere awaiting transmutation and attracting like energies and events. In this way the beneficent laws of karma impress upon us a sense of responsibility, even if only subconsciously. For good or ill the fire of thought draws together like energies to produce powerful living thought-forms, which influences the world in unseen ways. The karma of gossip, for example, is more deadly than is usually thought. **Beware of senseless condemnation. Not only does it contain the property of decomposition but it delivers the weak denunciator into the power of the condemned.** Thoughts of condemnation harm not only the one being condemned, but the greater harm is in the returning blow, which according to one estimate is increased to the power of ten.

---

[1] *Infinity* 1, 7

Psychic energy is, in one sense, the creative energy of thought. It is a manifestation of the one Sacred Fire or Primal Energy hidden within all beings. **Each of us carries within himself the One Fire, immutable throughout the entire universe. No one cares to imagine that the universal treasure is within him.**[1] Psychic energy is the fire of Manas (Universal Mind) the third principle of the divine trinity, Atma, Buddhi, Manas or to use Christian terminology Father, Son, and Holy Spirit (Mother). It is **the Breath of the Mother of the World,** the Light of spiritual Nature, who has ever veiled Her face from the eyes of man. The Mother of the World is primarily a principle rather than a being. And while this principle may be embodied by great Beings it is the principle that is of primary importance. +

Calling it psychic energy, we speak of the Sophia of the Hellenic world or Sarasvati of the Hindus. The Holy Ghost of the Christians manifests signs of psychic energy, just as do the creative Adonai of Israel, and Mithra of Persia, full of solar power. Certainly, no one doubts that the Fire of Zoroaster is the Fire of Space, which you now study.[2]

Psychic energy is the secret fire used by the alchemists to transmute one element into another. It is the secret ingredient in the workings of karma and the active ingredient behind all so-called psychic phenomena. Psychic energy manifests physically as the vital energy of all living organisms.

The question of how psychic energy is accumulated is justified. It is primarily accumulated **through the consciousness,** by paying attention to it. **The more such a quality is observed, the more it is developed. The fiery element loves to be noticed.**[3]

The Accumulation of psychic energy should be the most important goal, and all efforts must be directed toward this. Many insects—whether white or black—are drawn to the flame, for psychic energy is fire. One must understand that everything is attracted by psychic energy, and all measures

[1] *Fiery World* I # 7
[2] *Agni Yoga* 416
[3] *Fiery World* II, 90.

should be taken to utilize it properly.[1] Bothe co-workers and adversaries, visible and invisible, are drawn to the flame of psychic energy.

Descending into a deep cavern, one prefers to have a bright and even-burning lamp, rather than a smoky sputtering torch. It is the same with the quality of psychic energy. The sparks of a smoky flare do not improve a situation. But how to attain an even light? Only by constant meditation on the basic energy. Like a wordless mental process, in the rhythm of the heart, the inextinguishable Light is strengthened. Let hermits on the one hand and scholars on the other equally evaluate the light of the heart. Luminosity corresponds to an accepted degree of tension.

Whatever we place our attention upon grows stronger. This is one of the primary laws of yoga. To increase our store of psychic energy, or any quality we wish to develop, we must first give it close attention with a positive frame of mind. By watching closely the power and effect of thought, how it influences the thoughts of others, how it has the tendency to manifest itself, even physically, we increase its power. The sacred Fire is also accumulated through creative labor for the common good, through communion with Hierarchy, and by opening the heart to others.

Psychic energy can also be accumulated by observing closely the sensitivity of our feeling nature, distinguishing between emotions, which are always related to one's self, and feelings of the heart, which are always related to others. Look for the motives, the hopes and fears, behind the emotional energies as they arise. Fine-tune (refine and spiritualize) your feeling nature. Pure heart energy, which includes both wisdom and love, arises from the realization of selflessness, which is essentially the realization of unity. The unifying energy of the heart arises only in relation to others and our essential unity with them. Learn to distinguish the fine nuances of subtle feeling energies—solemnity, gratitude, devotion, and joy, paying particular attention to their causes, qualities, and strengths. The Teacher calls this the **education of the heart**. It entails intensifying one's feeling sensitivity through close observation and by striving to perceive clearly.

The attention should be intensified in order to observe the subtlest manifestations of the heart... He who has once listened to his heart does

_____

[1] *Agni Yoga* 567

not see any end to it. Observations that are begun in the home will inevitably guide the consciousness of him who observes universally and will indicate the path to the highest worlds. An observation of the subtle qualities of a refined feeling nature can always be raised to a higher power. Love for the birds or an individual, for example, can be raised to love for humanity.

Contact with the subtlest energies refines the entire being. He who has entered the fiery path understands the refinement, keenness, and vigilance of which I speak. In the education of the heart, unnoticeably to ourselves, we become accustomed to the spheres of the Subtle World. This occurs not because of some exceptional and miraculous phenomena but through minute sensations, which the sensitized heart begins to discern. One must acknowledge the idea of the significance of delicate sensations, but one should not become a bigot delving into the dogma of petty divisions. The heart will indicate the tortuous line between the vital and the conditional, between the natural and the unnatural. Gradually, little by little, we acknowledge that there exists about us a great number of manifestations that cannot be included in the laws of elementary physics. Experiences will increase, and an entire sequence of the sensations of the Subtle World will be brought together. This will be the most apparent beginning of the approach to the Subtle World. Following these sensations, we will begin also to accustom the physical body to the specific qualities of the next state. Penetrating into the essence of the laws of the Subtle World, we immediately gain specific steps in it. We consider it absolutely natural to accustom the consciousness to the subtle feelings in order thus to acquire physical adaptability.[1]

Where for whole years one exercised refinement and tempering of the body, [as in Hatha yoga] the heart can move the spirit almost immediately. Of course, the education of the heart is needed, but this lies in the sphere of feelings, not of [in bodily] mechanics.

We can increase our understanding of psychic energy through close observation during experiments. One can obtain almost immediate results by working with plants as they respond quickly to the power of thought. Take

---

[1] *Heart* 433

several plants of the same kind and of approximately the same age. Any species can be used. Place them in the same room and observe them yourself without showing any preferences. After two months separate the plants into three groups and place them in different rooms. Be indifferent toward the first group, send your good will to the second, and send your will for destruction to the third. These transmissions should be performed at a short distance and the rhythm of mahavan should be used.

It is helpful to have the length and intensity of these transmissions alternately increased and decreased every seven days. Three times daily is sufficient: morning, noon, and at sunset. In the morning the plants should be watered, adding a pinch of soda[1] to the water. At sunset they should be watered with a solution of valerian. One may continue in this way, testing the plants but also conditioning oneself to the performance of rhythmic action. Poisonous plants should not be used for these experiments, nor should any of the families of lilies or ferns. In this way the emanations of psychic energy will be increased.

Another experiment useful in the development of psychic energy pertains to energizing some character trait that we wish to develop within ourselves. By focusing our attention upon it in a positive manner we can greatly increase its activity. We must be careful with this, however, for by dwelling on the negative side of that habit we make it stronger.

The use of silent mantra is often helpful in experiments with psychic energy as it can help to establish a rhythm of thought. The power of mantra lies not so much in the physical sounds, but rather in the subtle vibrations produced by holding its essential meaning and intended purpose firmly in the consciousness. The physical sounds have no power of their own. Their power stems from the force of the psychic energy behind them. **Important are the succession of the layers of meaning, the sincerity of the direct transmission, and the rhythm... The developed consciousness can improvise words in accordance with the flow of psychic energy.**[2] The power of command is often assisted by laying on of the hands.

---

[1] Baking soda contains phosphors which plants love.
[2] *Agni Yoga*, 421

62

Other psychic energy experiments might include sending from the heart silent suggestions to the student or patient (without the imposition of will), projecting energy through the hands in healing, increasing the potency and effectiveness of natural medicines, magnetizing water or an object with special qualities, and by establish a link with a student or friend. The use of psychic energy is always greatly fascinated by adding a few drops of heart energy to the mix. Heart energy is refined psychic energy.

The true direction of research will be toward the study of both physical plane energies and the invisible energies that saturate space.[1] The laws of physics can be applied to the laws of psychic energy and visa versa. **Since psychic energy is energy it will not contradict the laws of physics.**[2]

To master psychic-energy, to purify and refine the consciousness, a certain amount of solitude is necessary. This must be found without withdrawing form life. This is the Middle Way. **The spirit of darkness pondering how to still more firmly lash humanity to the earth, thought: "Let them keep their old customs and habits. Nothing binds humanity so much as habitual forms. But this is fit only for the multitudes. Far more dangerous to us is solitude, in which the consciousness is illumined and new forms are created. People must not be allowed to remain alone. I shall provide them with a reflection so that they may become accustomed to being with their own image." Thus the servants of darkness brought a mirror to the people!**[3]

$\mathscr{P}$ray without ceasing," says Paul the apostle. **Pray without words,** says the Teacher. **The heart filled to the brim with love will be active, valiant, and will expand to its capacity. Such a heart can pray without words and can bathe in bliss.**[4]

Sometimes let your heart converse with the Higher World. This conversation can be held in many tongues. Perhaps the heart will gather in its memory hours from many lives. Perhaps the conversation will be a silent

---

[1] *Agni Yoga* 220
[2] *AUM* 487
[3] *Agni Yoga* 266
[4] *Hierarchy* 280

one, without precepts and advice, only ascending and strengthening in ascension; there may be the silence of gratitude or the silence of the power of readiness. The flame of the heart is kindled in striving toward unification with the Higher World. Only the heart will find the way to Hierarchy. The heart will strengthen itself by the power of the Highest.[1]

How then should one pray? One can spend hours in aspiration, but there may also be a prayer of lightning speed. Then instantaneously, without words, man can place himself in continuity with the whole chain into the Infinite.... Thus, in silence, without wasting time, one can receive a stream of refreshment.[2]

Solemnity, the refined feelings of the heart consciousness, naturally arises at the spirits first glimpse of the beauty of Reality. The radiance of solemnity indicates the highest achievement of the heart.[3] Solemnity combines in itself ecstasy, ascent, a defense against evil, and the turning toward Hierarchy. Thus solemnity is a salvation, but it must be absorbed and maintained.[4]

One of the primary exercises of Agni Yoga consists in silent communion with the spiritual world, with Hierarchy, with the Guru. This can take place like lightening or it can be developed into a lengthy one-pointed meditation. It can even be maintained through our one's daily activities. From spiritual communion arises a subtle and most beautiful exaltation of spirit, a calm solemnity filled with continuous joy. When communion is maintained as a nearly continuous practice it becomes a gateway to that expansion of consciousness, that exalted point of spiritual tension, where the ego vanishes. As yogis we have a responsibility to always keep this love exaltation alive in us.

Some people seek the higher link by continually uttering a mantra, at first orally, then mentally. Yet they forget that the most powerful link is through the fire of the heart, an illumination that needs no words or

---

[1] *Heart* 41
[2] *Leaves of Morya's Garden* Vol. 2 III: IV: I
[3] *Heart* 491
[4] *Heart* 525

thoughts. **It lives in the fiery heart and nothing can break this sacred bond.**[1] In silence—without words or thoughts.

How necessary at times is unification through silence. Nothing reacts more upon the heart as silence.[2] Spiritual silence is that utter stillness of the spirit that is attained through communion and unity with the divine. Not only is the chatter of extraneous thoughts temporally silenced, but the emotional outpouring of a separate self are also silenced. A wonderful joy remains. It is the responsibility of the yogi, we are told, to maintain this exaltation of the spirit. **One must accustom oneself to constant communion with Hierarchy.**[3]

In the Greek Mysteries communion with the Hierarchy was called Theurgy. The divine Iamblichus, the fourth century author of *The Life of Pythagoras* and *The Mysteries*, defined theurgy as "the art of establishing contact, through the practice of secret rites, with the invisible powers that bridge the distance between the Gods and man." "We gain a likeness to the gods," he continued, "by virtue of our constant associating with them, starting from our own imperfections, we gradually take on the perfection of the divine. No one enters into the likeness of the gods, even to a minimal degree, unless they are present and we are united with them." Proclus (412-485 AD) also used the term 'theurgy' to mean communion with the Hierarchy.

If you ask me what methods are befitting our times, I say, 'you must prepare yourselves for direct communion.'[4] **The consciousness that is directed to us is continually being refined.**[5] Through communion the spiritual sensitivity of the enlightened consciousness is awakened. Through communion the fiery aura and shield is strengthened. Through silent communion with the divine our spiritual evolution is intensified and accelerated. Through communion the guiding hand is made manifest. Through communion **egotism falls away and selflessness is kindled.**[6] Through communion with the Hierarchy one attains union with the Supreme. **Communion with Hierarchy gives, as it were, a new musical key**

---

[1] *Supermundane # 817*
[2] *Hierarchy* 401
[3] *Agni Yoga* 341
[4] *Fiery World* II, 236
[5] *Fiery World* II, 240
[6] *AUM* 121

65

to all our actions.[1] Communion with Hierarchy leads to cooperation with the plans of the Hierarchy. Through cooperation the yogi enters the ranks of the Knights of the Sacred Fire as coworkers in the Great Work of spiritual evolution.

Silent communion can take place at any time. It can even become more or less a continuous spontaneous activity throughout the day. **The ignorant may suppose that uninterrupted communion with Hierarchy can distract one from the work itself, but, on the contrary, constant communion with Hierarchy lends a higher quality to one's labor.**[2]

The keys to the practice of Agni Yoga are simple—refine the consciousness in the fire of the heart, apply the Teaching in life, openhearted striving, and communion and cooperation with the spiritual Hierarchy.

Neither concentration, nor command of will, but love for Hierarchy produces direct communion.

In spirit, upon the summit, man can partake of communion with the Higher Power.... The state of ecstasy produces an influx of super-earthly forces. If such tension has been established, it is possible to prolong this moment of bliss, **in other words, man may receive a continuous increase of forces. It is only necessary that the source of forces become constant and near to him.**[3]

During communion with the Higher World it is possible to observe that bent or crossed legs have a deep significance.[4]

Do not permit such communion to become a formal performance of duty. Forced effort will never produce a firm step, for the work in the subtle world must be a natural expression of free will. Do not try to force anyone to such labor, for desire for communion **must first be generated in the consciousness. It is difficult to judge when the desire to work for humanity will be ignited. Each one can find his path, and we will help those on that path.**[5]

---

[1] Fiery *World* III, 163
[2] *The Fiery* World II 118
[3] *AUM* 124
[4] *AUM* 122
[5] *Supermundane* 18

66

As the spiritual connection with the Teacher becomes strong, and trust and cooperation is established, there develops over time a mysterious overlapping of consciousness. This is called Paloria. **There can be an instantaneous coming together of the consciousness with the consciousness of the Teacher. One almost ceases to be aware of oneself, but the Chalice is filled to the brim with straight-knowledge [enlightenment] Such union surpasses words, for it nurtures one with straight-knowledge. Of course it is not easy to attain such a state. With an expansion of consciousness it comes by itself, if not hindered by ignorance.[1] Many fear to believe in the united consciousness. For them, each such union is an intrusion upon their selfhood, and as such is entirely intolerable. They will never appreciate the tenfold multiplication of energy born of the cooperation of consciousness. But without such cooperation the entire Teaching of the Heart would be impossible... If this principle is attainable, then it is likewise possible to extend it until it blossoms into the full unification of consciousness called Paloria.[2]** Paloria is defined as the unification and identification of the consciousness of the yogi with the divine Presence within all beings. The Hierarchy embodies this primordial nature for humanity until they can realize it themselves. Unity of consciousness involves no loss of identity, but rather a shift of identification from a false separate self to our true essential nature, which is at one with Hierarchy. As the personal can enter the kingdom of heaven we must transform the personal into the divine.

Sometimes we say, 'Strive to us with all your might.' Such a call may seem unusual, but those who know understand the urgency contained in it. It is not easy to concentrate upon one object. People may labor for many years to develop this ability. Success depends not on special abilities, but on intensified desire. Each one can try to strive to his Teacher, but he must strive so intently that he forgets all surroundings, whether it is day or night, warm or cold, for a short time or long. All this is within human power.[3]

---

[1] *Agni Yoga* 563
[2] *Heart 113*
[3] *Supermundane* 72

During morning meditation, perhaps while facing the rising sun, it is good to make an offering. The sincere dedication of one's time and energy to further the Great Work is always appropriate.

Strengthen my heart, oh Lord,
And give power to my arm,
For I am thy servant.
In thy Ray I shall learn the eternal truth of being.
In thy voice we shall listen to the harmony of the world.
Accept my heart's fire, oh Lord,
And sacrifice it for the sake of the world.

Perhaps your offering will be accepted. Perhaps it will be used along with others to divert a catastrophe. Perhaps your gift will aid someone unknown to you.

The urgency of the times requires unusual methods. In the past even the existence of the Brotherhood was kept secret. Now, at this time of transition between the old world and the new, between Kali Yuga and Satya Yuga, a time of extreme imbalances, much help is being given by the Brotherhood to rescue as many people as possible before certain deadlines.[1]

But in out search for the Hierarchy a word of warning must be given! Those who seek to obstruct the Evolution of Light, both knowingly and unknowingly, are literally flooding the Internet and the bookstores with so-called spiritual treasures that glitter brightly, but are in fact false and most deadly in their conclusions! Even initiates are sometimes fooled. Strive for discernment and clarity of vision!

All self-initiated activity through the school of life is accomplished by striving. Spiritual striving is an act of will, motivated by purified desire and the impulse behind Evolution. Striving attracts like a magnet those energies and qualities which correspond to our heart's desire. But striving should not

---

[1] See *Fiery World* I 121

be forced. It should arise as the natural inclination of the spirit in response to the attractive power of the very heart essence of our being. Striving magically and invisibly influences events. The pure striving of an open heart attracts spiritual energies, spiritual possibilities, and spiritual potencies. **A striving will, emanating from the fiery heart, produces a vortex drawing in corresponding energies.**[1]

The driving force behind cosmic evolution in the Teaching is called 'Fiery Impulse' and 'Currents of Evolution.' The goal of the Agni Yogi lies in cooperation with this Impulse. Through fiery striving and through refining the consciousness in the fire of the heart, the spiritual sensitivity of the yogi is awakened. He now perceives and acts creatively upon these divine impulses of the spiritual will. When the impulse meets with spontaneous response, the yogi's actions are said to be in step with the Evolution, he is 'in the Tao,' as we used to say. Now this may seem at first like the giving up our personal freedom, our independent sense of self. However, eventually it is realized that the Tao, the spiritual impulse behind evolution, originates from the very essence and core of our being, our true nature, our true identity. Thus identification shifts from the outer form to the inner spirit.

Personal will is transformed into spiritual will through cooperation with the evolution of Nature, physical and spiritual. The key word here is cooperation. Personal will is not suppressed or destroyed. Its actions are in step with the greater life of which it now perceives itself to be a part.

The freedom that so entices man is an illusion. It is generally thought that freedom means to do whatever we want. But in reality we are bound by our desires. True freedom is self-mastery, and this entails most particularly, mastery of our desire nature. True freedom is liberation from the strangle hold that desire has upon us. Ask someone who is fighting a crippling addiction, what freedom is.

Spiritual freedom means unobstructed activity. But what is it that most obstructs our way? It is our own emotional baggage—fear, personal desires, etc., plus a lack of self-control. These obstructions to spiritual freedom are removed through self-mastery.

---

[1] *Fiery World* III, 305

Food requirements are not complicated. The chief thing is to avoid blood, since it is an element, which introduces emanations unfit for the refined organism. But even in case of extreme necessity, one can avoid blood by using either dried or smoked meat. Similarly, in planning cereal or vegetable diets, one should be guided by the condition of one's organism. Yet even without yoga anyone can understand that any excess is harmful. And everyone knows about the vitamins in raw products.[1] Cooking, processing, pasteurization, and sterilization, all destroys the vitality, the pranic energy, naturally in food. Vegetables, fruit, milk, and cereals are always beneficial. People need little—two fruits, some cereal, and milk. Milk and honey are considered nutritious products, yet they have been entirely forgotten as regulators of the nervous system. When used in their pure [raw] form, they contain the precious primary energy. Precisely this quality in them must be preserved. Whereas, the sterilization (pasteurization) of milk and the special processing of honey deprive them of their most valuable property. There remains the nutritive importance, but their basic value disappears.[2] One should abstain from meat, except smoked meats. Vegetables, fruit, milk, and cereals are always beneficial. All alcohol is barred, except for curative purposes. Narcotics, such as opium, are inimical to Agni Yoga.

Some popular self-help books advise us to embrace our shadow self, to make friends with it, etc. This is a mistake! Self-mastery involves mastering the internal dragon. In the Ancient Mystery Schools the shadow self was called The Guardian of the Threshold to the Greater Mysteries. The candidate for initiation could not enter the higher Way without first mastering his shadow self.

One must be able not only to gaze into the Heights, but also to look into the depths of one's own nature. The latter is just as difficult as the former. The age-old serpent lies ready in the depths of the chalice, and will awaken and stir with any misstep. He fills one with malice; he saps one's

---

[1] *Fiery World* I 188
[2] *Brotherhood* 148

strength, and obscures good intentions. Only with great striving can one rid oneself of this ancient companion.[1]

It is not possible to remove all the heads of the hydra with one blow of the sword. It is said that each drop of blood begets new offspring! Therefore, one must find the way to cause the monster to die of hunger. Remove the monster's nourishment and it will disappear, crumbling into a handful of ashes.[2]

Whatever we think about we feed with our psychic energy. Therefore, constant vigilance is needed, to master our thoughts. To embrace the shadow-self is to feed it with our own life-energy.

The Path of the Heart must proceed naturally, without the application of force. Can the heart be force? Can union with the divine be forced? Austere measures of military like discipline only create more obstacles, for the act, to be natural, must reflect the attitude behind it. Can nonattachment be forced? To give away all our possessions, for example, will not eliminate our attachment to them. The Law of Attraction draws us forward naturally. The heart consciousness awakens naturally when the spirit is drawn toward the beautiful, to what is loved.

All unbalanced conditions must be eliminated naturally. Passionate imbalances cannot be arrested by command or by compulsion. Striving will build a firm bridge on the foundation of a refined consciousness. One must recognize the usefulness of this, then comes true evolution. But without realization it is impossible to overcome the lower earthly passions. Even if one gathers all the power of will, one still cannot evoke the Fire of Space. Those manifestations of the fiery element are not subject to command; they grow naturally from the expansion of consciousness.[3]

The Sacred Fire illuminates the consciousness in direct response to the yogi's pure heart felt striving for union with the divine. One can kindle the Spatial Fire only through the fire of the heart.[4]

---

[1] Supermundane 478
[2] Supermundane 480
[3] *Agni Yoga* 463
[4] *Fiery World* I # 30

A mirage does not disclose reality, but it is a reality itself. Therefore it is correct to recognize the reality of Maya with all its treacherous distortion.[1] To say that matter does not exist is false. It is an illusion, yes, merely a reflection of the higher planes, but it is a real reflection. The movie is not real life, but it is a real movie. According to Maitreya, the future Buddha, the essential nature of phenomena is real while its appearance in form is not.[2] It is only an illusion when its essential nature is not perceived. An illuminated consciousness perceives the mutual interdependence of the relative with the universal. This the Buddha taught.

Some may be unable to reconcile the existence of equality with the Hierarchy. Equality is contained in the potentiality of spirit. Hierarchy holds the irreplaceability of tested accumulations.[3] Spiritual paradoxes of the kind can be understood when it is realized that two levels are being expressed, relative and universal. For some this seems to be a contradiction. When Lincoln said, 'All men are created equal,' he was referring to the 'potentiality of spirit,' and not to the numerous unequal grades of people according to their 'tested accumulations.' The same kind of paradox can be found in the popular statement that 'its all perfect.' The statement is true only as 'the potentiality of spirit.' It is false when applied the 'tested accumulations' of our present station on the path. It is harmful when applied to every day life for it prevents striving for perfection. In essence we are equal. In expression we are not. Our unchanging essential nature is perfect. Its expression on the Path that leads to perfection is not.

Beyond the range of one's conscious thought flows a constant unconscious interaction, embracing wide circles, limited by the law of karma and affinity of auras.[4] The mysterious arising of events involving the relationships of people are not as random as they seem, if random at all. They are produced by causes that are conditioned by the laws of attraction and karma. The

---

[1] *Agni Yoga* 288
[2] See *The Essential Teachings of Maitreya*, Pentarba Publications 2019. Pentarba.com
[3] *Agni Yoga* 5
[4] *Agni Yoga* 168

attraction of kindred spirits as well as the attraction of karmic events, are conditioned by the quality and nature of the psychic energy of the auras of the individuals involved. The term aura, as used in this verse and elsewhere in the Teaching, depicts not only the radiation of the energies of the ethereal body, but the radiations of psychic energy of the astral and mental bodies as well. The invisible working of the laws of attraction is great mystery for it deals with the way in which co-workers and dear friends find each other and how karmic events are so accurately brought about.

Tension, as the term is used in the Teaching, does not refer to the stress of emotional tension or even physical tension, but rather an intensity of psychic energy. **When I indicated tension, I had in mind not muscular tension, but that of the heart.**[1] Pure striving, solemnity, gratitude, and communion with Hierarchy, all intensify the psychic energy. **Spiritual tension accumulates spatial psychic energy.**[2] From this spiritual tension arises the powers and straight-knowledge of the saints. **He who has directed his vision toward infinity understands that the higher it is the greater the tension. Thus prepare people for an inevitable intensification.**[3] An intensification of heart energy is necessary to the spiritual Path! This may seem to be at first a bit uncomfortable, but once the emotional stability of a calm spirit is realized, this tension is experienced as bliss. All the great yogi-saints, all the great servers, feel this spiritual tension. **The calm of the yogi is as the tension of an ocean wave.**

The Aum represents the subtle vibration arising from the spiritual tension generated by the fiery heart essence of the Supreme. **Some imagine it as a loud sound whereas the sound may be inaudible like the heart's tension; for it is the heart that sings. It resounds and the entire organism is filled with a special energy.** In the scriptures of India the yogi is instructed to listen for the subtle sound originating from the heart essence of his being. When perceived, and its meaning realized, it may then be sounded silently. But the **sound may be rightly understood and still produce no results.**

---

[1] *Heart* 186
[2] *Agni Yoga 509*
[3] *Heart* 314

73

Therefore, let us not forget the heart's energy, which must accompany the sound. In this way the Aum becomes a conduit for communion with the spiritual world.

One should be not surprised if in speaking of prayer emphasis is put on the need to be mindful of vibratory conditions. Such investigation of all the attributes of communion with the Higher World will be the true path.[1]

The sacred Fire, drawn down from above through the striving of an open heart, gives a powerful creativeness to those thoughts that further spiritual evolution. **The coordination of the trend of thought with created affirmations** for the common good **stratifies space with the manifestations of Spatial Fire.** The Sacred Fire thus becomes a fiery incentive, an impulse to create according to the plan as indicated by the Teaching. This creative impulse, however, is given only in essence. It lies with the coworkers, in full freedom, to supply the details, to interpret and thereby individualize the work for the benefit of the world. The covenant of Christ states, **By human hands and feet will the new Temple of the Lord be built.** Without the freedom to express the incoming spiritual energies creatively there would be no individual freedom. **Freedom is valuable for guarding the personality and for the individualization of the attracted energies.**

In this we must tread the Middle Way between independent action and obedience to the spiritual will. This may at first seem like contradictory concepts, but when the freedom of independent action finds harmonious cooperation with the divine will unity is maintained without loss of identity or individuality. **Humanity must learn to act independently and to embody all the thoughts by the Teacher.** "There is no contradiction," writes the great Plotinus, "between destiny and free choice. Destiny includes free choice."

Independent action, which is primarily independent thinking, means action that is not conditioned by outside sources. In the last analyses, the spiritual Will is not an outside source. It is a part of our true essential nature. By uniting with the Teacher, who embodies that Will, we are uniting with the divine essence that moves all life toward perfection.

---

[1] *AUM* 50

Independent thinking that is not conditioned by the mass mind is difficult to attain. We must learn to question everything, not as the skeptic who gravitates toward denial, but with an open mind. We must develop the determination to see the truth for ourselves, independent of all outside authority, including the authority of the Teaching. When the truths of the Teaching are verified through our own experience then belief is transmuted into insight.

At some point on the path the seeming paradox between personal freedom and divine will must be resolved. But this involves a refined spiritual sensitivity. **He who adheres to the Teaching of Infinity gains freedom of action first of all.**[1]

Sleep or vigilance, labor or rest, motion or repose, all carry us equally toward the fulfillment of life's plan. 'It is like fallen leaves,' say the timid. It is like seeds for the sowing,' say the wise. 'It is like arrows of light,' say the daring. The Knights of the Sacred Fire direct their thoughts, as arrows of light, to the fulfillment of life's plan.

The Teacher warns the students against the practice of magic. But, as we have seen, this does not include the seemingly miraculous activity created through the application of psychic energy. This is not only encouraged but is considered a necessary aspect to the spiritual evolution of humanity for the coming Epoch of Maitreya. **Let us recall, someone reacted to cosmic manifestations; someone heard far-off voices; someone, envisioning it, participated in the Subtle World; someone became luminous; someone levitated; someone walked upon the water; someone walked through fire; someone swallowed poison without harm; someone had no need of sleep; someone had no need of food; someone could see through solid bodies; someone could write with both hands; someone could attract animals; someone could understand a language without knowing it; someone could read thoughts; someone could read with closed eyes a closed book; someone did not feel pain; someone in the snow generated the heat of the heart; someone did not feel fatigue; someone could help by healing;**

---

[1] *Hierarchy* 29

someone could manifest knowledge of the future. Thus, one can enumerate all manifested phenomena and a multitude of instructive examples from life. But for an instant gather all these qualities into one body and you will have the new human transmutation indicated in many Teachings.

The magic that the Teaching warns us against refers to the ritual invocation of elementals and astral entities. Elementals are the spirits of of the material elements. They are powerful and as they have very little will of their own, they can be manipulated by the strong will of the magician. Astral entities are discarnate human and deva beings that live on the astral plane, the plane of desire and emotions. These are the ones usually contacted by psychics. The invocation of these entities is considered unnatural and therefore harmful to evolution. One must picture to oneself how in this manner entities of the lower strata obtain access into forbidden spheres and continue to work harm on a broad scale. That is why extensive measures are needed in order to safeguard the planet, which is sick enough as it is. Magic in general must be left alone.[1]

One should not seek afar that which is near. What irreparable harm to humanity results from the extensive searches into magic! Instead of working to improve their consciousness, seekers limit themselves to repeating formulas of others, without any knowledge of their meaning and rhythm. What is so inimical to evolution as the petrified formulas of magic? The astral world has been separated from the physical world most of all by the ways of magic. Of course, possession is often the result of magical invocations. Mediumism is the bedfellow of magic. The magic formulas that have been given out to the public are intentional distortions. In them some things are missing that were reserved for oral transmission. Certainly a yogi is the very opposite of a magician. A magician stands on petrified formulas. A yogi constantly inhales the fresh new breath of Cosmos. The one is old at birth; the other is always young, throughout all changes in his life. The one attempts to strike with words not of his own making; the other smites with his free thought. The one defends himself with pitiful pinpricks; the other is shielded just by the armor of his glance. Yoga has nothing in common with magic.[2]

---

[1] *Fiery World* II, 306
[2] *Agni Yoga* 233

Invocations and incantations can of course help in attuning oneself to the spatial rhythm, but the law of evolution presumes a more direct contact of the human consciousness with the cosmic one. Instead of the rhythm of magic formulas one should comprehend the fiery seed of the spirit and silently build the bond linking the fire of one's spirit with the Fire of Space.[1]

The currents of evolution are cosmic rays streaming forth from the spiritual world providing the impulse behind the evolution of the human spirit and all life on this planet. Cooperation with the work of the Hierarchy is in direct alignment with these cosmic seeds. The Knights of the Sacred Fire also sends out rays, thought currents that contain those psychic seeds useful for the hastening of spiritual evolution.

On the last earthly step before the victorious crowning, conformity of the fiery transmuted centers with the cosmic Ray is established. Each perceivable tension of the centers has its corresponding cosmic designation. Thus the centers are saturated with fire for the admittance of the great cosmic Ray, which adepts all the vehicles for the final rending from the Earth. The physical, subtle, and astral bodies thus take on one and the same image of beauty... In this lies the supreme cosmic mystery and the greatest manifestation of cosmos.[2]

Yoga (union with the divine) is achieved through self-mastery. This entails the discipline, purification, and refinement of our thoughts and feelings. The appearance of unfit thoughts could be eradicated at once, but people are such that they listen without hearing and do not read beyond the sight.[3] To discipline the thoughts we must first pay close attention to them. For this vigilance is needed. This watchfulness can be developed through one pointed meditation. Usually, people are enslaved by their thoughts; and nothing so impedes advancement as grievous immobile thoughts.

---

[1] *Agni Yoga* 321
[2] *Fiery World* III, 31
[3] *Heart* 16

One must become accustomed to the fact that each thought is a communion with Fire. Hence, it is shameful to have an ignorant or insignificant thought.[1]

By mastering our thoughts and feelings we gain the power to resolve many of the difficulties of the path. That a situation is without solution is only imagined by those who would rely on other people rather than upon the power of their own thoughts.

How carefully the disciples must define the quality of their thoughts! Has not the worm of selfhood or self-conceit or the manifestation of self-love hidden somewhere? Honest avowal of such is something that each spirit must develop within himself.[2]

It is not so easy to learn to think. It is difficult to develop the tension of thought, but still more difficult to attain a high quality of thought. Often mentally a man repeats to himself, "I will think purely," But his being is accustomed to egotistic thinking. Then the most undesirable form of thought results. Two birds flying from different nests cannot become united as one. It is necessary to exercise thought, not mentally but with the fire of spirit, until all duplicity of thought disappears.[3]

Karma is the result of the freewill creative activity of the mind that is not in harmony with the currents of evolution. Dharma is activity of the mind that is in harmony with the flow of evolution. Evolution requires the transmutation of accumulated karmic energies.

The laws governing karma are good as they highlight our mistakes and teach us responsibility. By actively striving to overcome the negative effects of our thoughts we progress on the path. Karma and transmutation constitute factors that direct us toward progress. They create their effect by the propulsion of karma and they set the direction by the transmutation of the spirit.[4]

---

[1] *Fiery World* I 33
[2] *Agni Yoga* 661.
[3] *Agni Yoga 345*
[4] *Infinity* II 62 & 63

Cosmic evolution gives the fiery impulse to ascend in spirit through the law of attraction. Karma propels the spirit forward through the law of repulsion.

Liberation is freedom from the chains of karma. The transmutation of crystalized karmic energies takes place through the agency of the fire of the heart. **Only when the spirit strives to the pure Fire** of Spirit **can the shells be transmuted.**[1]

The spirit that has discerned the substance of karma aspires to liberate the seed of spirit **from its encasing shells. These shells gather like mist around the seed. Each seed goes through its battle** for liberation from the karmic shells **on its way to the Infinite.**[2]

The absolute is not contained in the transitory form, but the spirit of the form, the seed, **expresses the Absolute... The shell of the cosmic seed in its transmutation is subject to the law of time, but the spirit of the seed endures beyond time.**

To break the laws of life is to create suffering for oneself and others. Karma (divine justice) is good for it propels us to transmute the impure energies we have created in order to free ourselves from suffering. **Karma propels the spirit toward its destination.... Karma presses upon the heels of human ascent.**[3] **Karma and** its **transmutation constitute the factors that direct** us **toward progress.**[4]

The guiding star is karma, affirmed by the actions of many lives.... The guiding star will be that skiff which conveys one to the other shore amid the raging elements.[5]

The Law of Attraction *draws* us ever forward toward perfection. The Law of Karma *propels* us forward toward the goal.

*T*wo **paths exist—the path of analysis and the path of synthesis.**[6] H. P. Blavatsky called these two paths 'the Eye Doctrine and the Heart

---

[1] *Infinity* II 71
[2] *Infinity* II 70
[3] *Infinity* II 65
[4] *Infinity* II # 63
[5] *Fiery World* III, 82
[6] *AUM* 133

79

Doctrine,' the way of the rational mind and the way of the wisdom of the heart. Analysis divides that which is being investigated into its component parts to better understand the way things works. Modern science follows this approach. The path of synthesis, the holistic approach, looks for the unity and essential nature of things and always in relation to the greater whole. The Pythagorean School combined both methods of approach. First the monad, the essential unity of any whole system or organism was perceived, and then how it related to other organisms and the greater whole. According to Maitreya, the coming Buddha, both paths (the relative and the non-relative) are necessary for the enlightenment and perfection of the human consciousness.[1]

Religion and science are but two ways of approaching an understanding of the same truths. Religion works from above down, while science reasons from below upward. The time is approaching when they will meet, and the Middle Path will be more broadly recognized. **Religion and science must not be considered separate in their essential nature. A subtle study of matter and the atom leads to the conclusion that vital energy is not electricity but** a subtle divine **Fire. Thus science and religion merge upon a single principle. Matter is affirmed as a fiery substance, and no thoughtful spirit will deny that the higher force is** a spiritual **Fire. Science cannot destroy the concept of the divinity of Fire, nor can any religion impose an interdiction on the subtle analyses made by science. In this way, then, the understanding and the harmony of the concepts of religion and science are affirmed. A subtle parallel can be drawn between science and religion, which will reveal all the higher stages.[2]** When Einstein demonstrated the matter was nothing but energy he was pointing toward this divine unity.

The intellect (*manas*) is downward moving—creative. Its nature is to divide and separate, to analyze, and to manifest into form. The fire of the heart (*bodhi*) is upward moving. Its nature is to unify, to synthesize, to abstract (liberate) from the form. We can direct our attention, activity, and energy in either of these two directions as needed. The Middle Path finds the

---

[1] See *The Essential Teachings of Maitreya*, Pentarba Publications, 2019 Pentarba.com
[2] *Fiery World* III, 60

80

balance point between these two directions—creative service and striving to the heights. Its symbol is the cross.

The keynote of the Teaching is Synthesis. For this reason it is difficult to make an organized dogmatic religion out of it. Fixed divisions are rare. Terms like primal and psychic energy, for example, are to be understood holistically, as one all-pervading Fire. From the perspective of synthesis there are no boundary lines of separation between biological energy (prana), the energy of the centers, the energy of the thought and feeling, the refined fire of the heart, and the currents of evolution or rays (cosmic thought energy). Teachings given in this way leads to the realization of oneness.

With synthesis naturally arise thoughts of simplicity and beauty. **Simplicity, beauty, and fearlessness, the Christ and the Buddha spoke of nothing more.[1] Simplicity is the key to the secret door of happiness.[2] If you can express the most lofty is a brief way, do so.**

*I*mpetuousness is valuable when it is the result of full consciousness.[3] To be impetuous means to act on impulse. Maitreya tells us in his *Teaching on the Buddha Nature*[4] that the actions of the Buddha were always spontaneous, without pre-meditation, in others words he acted, in full consciousness, on the impulse of spirit.

*Th*e symbol of the spiral is laid at the foundation of our creative power.[5] The spiral is the path which all energy naturally follows as it moves through space. This is true for subtle energy as well as physical. A planet, for example spirals through space, as does the psychic energy of thought, as does our path to the higher worlds. When the physicist declares that light follows the pattern of a wave it means that only the dense or lower half of the spiral has being detected. The power of directed energy is produced by a continual repetition of energy impulses. The energy continuously repeats itself on each

---

[1] *Leaves of M's Garden* 2, 132
[2] *Leaves of M's Garden* 2, 131
[3] AUM 560
[4] See *The Essential Teachings of Maitreya*, Pentarba Publications 1019. Pentarba.com
[5] The following verses on the spiral are from *Infinity* I, 114. Also see my *Gates of Infinity*. Pentarba.com

turn of the spiral so that a precise rhythm is created. Thus the energy builds in its intensity and power.

The gradual growth does not permit creativeness to wane. When growth naturally follows the intended spiral course, the rhythm of the evolutionary impulses insures its constructive manifestation. According to this natural law of motion it is easy to see why the pattern of the spiral manifests in all natural growth.

Who then will manifest the spiral motion if not those who are united in the highest blending! This involves the realization of synthesis, enlightenment, a uniting of the consciousness with the fiery impulse behind the evolution of spirit.

The rhythm of the spiral accelerates proportionately with the ascent. It is the motion of the spiral that gives rhythm, the ebb and flow, to the manifesting evolutionary current. The greater the degree of our ascent, the closer we come to spiritual union, the greater the intensity of energy. As evolution is thus accelerated so do the cycles of change increase their pace and creative intensity.

The factor of time, which is so great a burden to humanity, can be understood in the radiance of the power of motion of the creative spiral. Time moves forward in the spiral. It is this motion that gives to evolution its cycles of change, its ebb and flow, its Kali Yugas and its Satya Yugas. As evolution accelerates so do the cycles of change in time, until the shift in consciousness is understood more in terms of dimension than speed. By understanding the spiral of creation we can gain some understanding of the spiral of evolution, and visa versa.

People are in dread of time, realizing the crumbling of their structures. This is because man manifests motion without rhythm. Rhythm is created when each turn of the spiral is in sync with the previous turn. This consistency gives duration to the created patterns. The cyclic rhythms of Nature give a good example of this. The objective is to apply this natural law to the spiritual path.

The beauty of the spiral tension will be at the base of all creativeness. Cosmos manifests to the spirit that spiral. Materia Lucida at the disposal of

the blended heart will manifest the highest forms of Beauty.[1] Creativeness of spirit, in sync with evolution, creates with materia lucida, matter that is radiant with energy. It is at the disposal of the creator who has blended his heart with the Heart Essence of the Cosmos. When this is the case the creations will be beautiful.

The secret fire of the alchemists, the agency used to transmute one state or condition into another higher state, is psychic energy. The following somewhat veiled verses from *Infinity* 1, 42 & 55, pertain to alchemical transmutation.

The assimilation of higher energies, upon the evidence of tension, can give form to new energies. Matter and spirit grow through mutual help. When the tensed current of will flows with accelerated speed, matter is absorbed by the spirit and the functions of a spiritual creator are performed. Then the refining of form takes place. The power of the fire of spirit is like the power of the fire that melts metals. Only through the process of melting may one form new combinations. That spirit who yearns to bring his energy into incandescence becomes a melter of matter. What forms and dimensions the spirit can melt, from all the spatial matter from our lives! From times immemorial the Lords have assumed the task of melting the consciousness.

Through the consistent upward striving of a fiery heart and a focused will held at a point of tension upon the goal, a certain spiritual intensity of consciousness is produced. This attracts the sacred Fire of space, which when combined with the accumulated fire of consciousness transforms the spirit into a higher state. The evolution of spirit and matter occurs through their mutual interaction and cooperation. The transformation of the spirit follows the same laws as the transmutation of matter and energy. The function of a spiritual creator is to reduce (melt) matter to its primary essential nature through the application of the secret fire. This is matter being absorbed by the spirit. When the form has been transmuted to its primary essence, it can then be built upon to create new forms. This can also be

---

[1] Infinity 1, 114.

applied to the evolution of consciousness, 'as above, so below.' Through assimilation of the higher energies consciousness becomes illuminated, radiant with the spiritual light. This highly intensified spiritual energy can then be used to transmute the imperfections in our lives by reducing them to their undistorted original nature. To melt the consciousness means to reduce (raise) it to its essential nature, the root source and origin of consciousness itself (*Alaya*).

A limited consciousness attracts only imperfect currents. The power of creativeness responds to the call of the spirit, and the scope of consciousness corresponds to the surrounding conditions created by the spirit itself. The law of reaction is the most recti lineal. Cosmic energy as a propelled creative impulse will provide a culminating life there where striving is manifest. If man would comprehend the great mutual attraction, he would more often propel his energy toward cosmic creativeness. The call is affirmed as a great magnet. The belief that the evocation "AUM" is effective, when consciously made by the spirit, is based on wisdom. But the spirit invoked by an irresponsible spirit can only smite. All causes and effects are contained in the call.

The spirit of the one who invokes arouses and summons the cosmic power. The spirit who calls Infinity to the aid of humanity becomes the helper of evolution. The spirit who knows not the call will not utilize the manifest forces of Infinity.[1] Fiery striving and the call attract, like a magnet, the power of cosmic creativeness. But this creativeness is dependent upon the state of our consciousness at the time. AUM is the call. It becomes effective through confidence in its power and through the realization of the mutual attraction that exists between the striving spirit and the fiery impulse of spirit. The call must be made in full consciousness and with a full sense of responsibility. Otherwise the fire will smite the caller. It must be used only to aid humanity and to further the Great Work of evolution.

---

[1] *Infinity 1, 55*

It is an error, says the Zen master, to mistake the finger pointing at the moon for the moon itself. The religion, philosophy, or teaching that one follows is merely pointing to the Way. It is not the Way itself. The best Teachings are pointing to a truth that can only be realized through experience. Memorizing the words or forms of the scriptures may be useful but they will not take the place of direct perception. For the rational mind it is easier to understand the letter of the law than the spirit of truth behind it. The best teachings become traps when we turn them into a fixed dogma. When this happens all other forms but the one we have embraced will seem false. Even the same truth spoken in the words of another teaching will seem false. This can happen even with the highest teachings.

The Path is not ever confined to one philosophy, teaching, or religion. Therefore seek the truth of other teachings than your own. Weigh and compare and don't fall into the trap of fanaticism and limiting dogma. This is the experience of synthesis as it applies to yoga.

My dear friend Millen, once said, "Look for the truth wherever you can find it, but choose one path and follow it all the way."

We are reminded many times of the need to apply the Teaching in life. In this labor the will is developed. **Each of our indications helps to open the gate. However there is no indication that does not require labor for its fulfillment.**[1] This is difficult for it involves the voluntary will, self-initiated discipline of spirit. **We return many times to this concept of voluntariness. It is the foremost condition of discipline. The least thought about forcing destroys all achievements. Not only does the Teacher not compel, but the disciple also must not force himself. The discipline of Good is a self-generated joy.**[2] The will is developed through voluntary creative labor that is in step with the evolution. The heart knows this direction. **Only the blind are unable to perceive the direction of evolution.**[3]

One should remember that the cultivation of the will is the best aid for the attainment of illumination, bursting into flame it shines like a torch,

---

[1] *Supermundane* 438
[2] *Supermundane* 559
[3] *Agni Yoga* 49

85

revealing the Path. But how does one develop the will? Perhaps with the aid of concentration or pranayama. Every aid is useful. But the strongest will is shaped by the lessons of life.

The human mind flows by the command of the will and it is awareness of this that opens the gate. The will is thus developed by taking control of the mind. Without this we remain ever a slave to the wayward activity of our thoughts and emotions. Control of the mind is impossible without vigilance and will. **Everyone is hindered by something, but the power of the will can overcome anything.**[1]

The will is developed through the labor of self-mastery. Labor for self-perfection is not, in itself, a selfish action as it is in line with the natural evolution of consciousness. One of the stumbling blocks against the labor of developing of the will is the idea that work is something to be avoided. This unfortunate attitude may be due in part to the idea that labor means 'working for wages' with all the drudgery and exploitation that this usually entails. Labor, as the term is used in the Teaching, is creative, useful, beautiful and freely given for the sake of the world. The will is only developed through self-initiated labor. The spiritual will is developed when there is a spontaneous heart felt response and identification with the activity of the fiery creativeness of spirit.

One cannot name anyone who, without broadening the consciousness, can find joy in endless labor. Only our people will understand how life is fused with labor, drawing from it strength of achievement.... Seeking the Yoga of Fire, people must understand that the inner fire must be ignited by labor.[2]

The joy of labor arises from the realization of its creativeness, that something beautiful is being added to the treasury of life.

Buckminster Fuller, an original thinker of extraordinary insight, in the opening lines of his book, *The Critical Path*, says that the world crisis that we are moving ever deeper into, is 'brought about by cosmic evolution irrevocable intent upon completely transforming humanity' from separate

---

[1] *Supermundane 573*
[2] *Agni Yoga 347*

competing entities into an integrated harmonious whole. The crisis that is upon us is due primarily to resistance to the currents of Evolution. **Spatial currents, beneficial in essence can be destructive when they contact the foul atmosphere of the Earth.**[1] The atmosphere spoken of here refers to the psychic atmosphere created by human selfishness, irritation, malice, and anger.

The Earth is sick.[2] **Healing and cleansing measures are needed for the Earth. The infected layers must be purified and only man can do it.**[3] **One must restore the health of the Earth. By innumerable ways, one must carry out the world task of regeneration. One must bear in mind that people have destroyed the resources of Earth without mercy. They are ready to poison the earth and the air. They have decimated animal life, forgetting that animal energy nourishes the earth. They believe that untried chemical compounds can take the place of prana and earthly emanations. They plunder the natural resources, unmindful that the balance must be maintained. They do not ponder over the cause of the catastrophe of Atlantis. They do not consider the fact that chemical ingredients must be tested over the course of a century, for a single generation cannot determine the symptoms of evolution or involution. People like to calculate races and sub-races, but the very simple idea of calculating the plundering of the planet never occurs to them. They think that by some act of mercy the weather will clear, and people will become prosperous! But the problem of restoring health does not enter their thoughts. Hence, let us love all creation!**[4]

The channels of beneficence and the recipients of the earthly poison—thus are called the chosen ones, ready to offer themselves for the benefit of the world. The assimilation of the poison is unbearable without

---

[1] *Supermundane 413*

[2] *Agni Yoga* 334

[3] *Supermundane 413*

[4] *Fiery World I*, 630.

87

the power of Bliss. But without the earthly poison the power of Bliss would carry one away; thus striving upward has an earthly foundation.[1]

In the ancient *Bhagavata Purana* there is an allegorical story in which Lord Shiva appeared to the disciples with a throat black from the poison he had consumed for the behalf of the world. Through communion with Hierarchy the 'chosen ones' become recipients of the 'beneficence' of heaven. This stimulates and expands the consciousness to the point where it becomes extremely sensitive not only to the energies of spiritual worlds but also to the poisonous psychic energy that human beings are continuously creating in the world. This pollution ranges from the obvious physical pollution to the much more devastating pollution of cruelty, greed, crude thoughts, unhealthy desires and negative emotion. One cannot hear the Music of the Spheres, we are told, without also hearing the wailing cry of suffering humanity. Those with the acute sensitivity of an open heart strongly feels these earthly poisons and is affected by them. Through compassion for suffering humanity the Bodhisattvas of all degrees 'offer themselves as a sacrifice for the benefit of the world.'

Of course, the assimilation of poison is unbearable for many, but for the affirmation of Bliss an actual tempering of the heart is needed. We consider it a treasure when the heart is ever ready to resound to the environment, being already without tension. It is not easy to do this unless the energies are transformed in the heart into resounding crystals; then **there will be formed the *Ringse* so correctly pointed out in Tibet in the Covenant of the Himalayas.**

'Ringsel' (*Sarira* Sk.) is the Tibetan term for the secret pearl colored crystals of psychic energy that are formed in the body near the heart center and are sometimes found in the ashes after the cremation of the body of a great mahasiddha, lama, or saint.[2] They are **sediments of precipitated crystals, consisting of subtle energies that have been chemically transformed in the organism.**[3] **The Tibetan 'ringse' has a deep significance, being the sediment crystallized by the manifestation of bliss.**[4] The Tibetans

---

[1] *Heart 32*
[2] See *The Life of Milarepa*. Translated by Lobsang P. Lhalungpa, Boulder 1984, p.220.
[3] Fiery World III # 218
[4] *Hierarchy* 422. Also see Heart 120 & 354. See also the Agni Yoga Glossary below.

called these crystals Secret Bodhichittas, and Wish-fulfilling Gems. The Rosicrucians called them Philosopher's Stones, as they were stones created within the body of the philosophers. It was highly sought after by the alchemists. **Crystals of psychic energy, when applied to one's body, draw one's own inner psychic energy** into manifestation, **just as a magnet draws a needle from the body. One can imagine how powerful are crystals of psychic energy when used as medicines. They attract electronic particles of Teros from space. The emanations of the approaching waves surround one and color with their chemistry the attracted particles of energy. This is the chemical basis of so-called colored stars.**[1]

Friends, while the climb is difficult the view from the top is beautiful and wondrous to behold. If you remain steadfast in your ascent you will reach a point where even a reprimand will be cherished as evidence of the guiding hand. The Teacher will rarely communicate with us with many words. It may be that one word, pregnant with meaning, will, like lightning, penetrate the consciousness, but discourses are rare. Most often, usually as a confirmation of a true thought, you will feel the touch of the Teacher as unexpected feelings of pure bliss. This may be of short or long duration. Sometimes, during communion, a ray of understanding is given saturated with the high vibration of the Teacher.

If, at times, it seems to you that you have lost your higher connection, look first to your thought-life for the cause. It is important that we learn to be fully conscious of our thoughts and feelings, even to the point of changing their content, quality, and direction on command. Learn to expel with a sharp out breath any thought or emotion that is unfit for the goal of union. This is particularly important if you suspect that the thoughts originate from an outside source. When the Teacher reminds us to be vigilant it means to maintain a constant watchfulness over our thoughts and feelings. Remember always that thought is creative! By thinking of the future we create it! By dwelling on our problems, whether personal or national, we

---

[1] *Agni Yoga* 594-595

stimulate them. Give thought to the future, to the coming New World. As a man thinketh as a soul so is it!

My Counsels are analogous to a father's farewell to a departing son. The trunk for the voyage must contain objects for all conditions of life; but in the secret place is hidden the heart, and for a long time I shall still call after you, "Chiefly guard the secret place!"[1]

---

[1] *Heart* 521

Agni Yoga Glossary

Words in *italic* indicate that there is an individual listing under this heading. Sentences in **bold type** are quotations taken directly from the Teaching.

Abhidharma—A Sanskrit term combining abhi or highest, with dharma, the Way.[1] **The light of abhidharma is the combination of the fire of higher spheres with the radiant emanations of the consciousness.** This is the unity of the Sacred *Fire of Space* with *psychic energy.* **We demonstrated by example the protection that the light of Abhidharma provides against the poisoned emanations of the lower earthly strata.**[2]

Abramram—The Fire in the Chalice. Abhramram is a Sanskrit term which combines 'Abhram,' meaning a water bearer or cup, with 'Ram,' which is the seed syllable for fire. The *Chalice* is a secret center into which the Sacred Fire descends bringing illumination (radiance) of the consciousness. **Many people have observed the significance of the successive development of the centers. Incomprehensible labels often have been given to real things. Thus, when you hear the word Abramram it will be a reminder about the center of the Chalice, where straight-knowledge, predestined for the future evolution, is concentrated.** See *The Chalice.*

Achievement—Selflessness.

---

[1] Dharma, as the term is used in Buddhism is an abbreviation Buddha-dharma, meaning the Way as taught by the Buddha.
[2] *Agni Yoga* 498

Affinity—Also called **law of the magnet** and **the attractive power of the heart**. This principle, which is fundamental to the workings of cosmos, pertains to the Law of Attraction, which unites spirits of mutual kinship. The mystery of the affinity between kindred spirits is so beautiful. Also called *Concordance*.

Agni—The oldest and most revered of the Gods of India. He embodies the principle of the creative Fire of Manas or mind known in the Teaching as *psychic energy*. According to the Bhagavata Purana Agni embodies "The Sacred Fire hidden at the heart of all beings."[1] **Each of us carries within himself the One Fire, immutable throughout the entire universe. No one cares to imagine that the universal treasure is within him. The fire of the heart alone unites all world structures through its magnet.[2] Beautiful is the law that permits each incarnate being to have within him eternal Agni, as a Light in the darkness.[3]**
Also see *Primary Energy, Psychic Energy* and the *Fire of Space.*

Agni Invisibilae—A ray of silence sent by the Teacher to the disciple. **These rays are sent to the heart, invisibly and imperceptibly. They are most penetrative, and the organism must assimilate them. At first they evoke anguish, yet they are comparable to pure Fire. The one who sends experiences a manifestation of the highest joy, and the one who receives will manifest the same joy after assimilation.**[4]

Agni Yoga—**The perception and application in life of the all-embracing element of Fire, which nourishes the seed of the spirit.**[5] Agni Yoga is the **Yoga of the Realization of Fiery Power.**[6] *Agni* is the *Sacred Fire.* Yoga is the path leading to union with the divine. Agni Yoga unites the spirit with the divine *Sacred Fire.* Through heartfelt striving to unite with the divine we attract a portion of the *primal energy,* the *Fire of Space,* which illuminates the consciousness, activates and transmutes the energy of the centers, and becomes the connecting link with the essential nature of reality. **Only a**

---

[1] Skandha 7:11 An abridged translation has been recently produced by Ramesha Menon and published by Rupa Publishing.
[2] *Fiery World* I, 7
[3] *Fiery World* 1, 183
[4] *Infinity* I, 81
[5] *Agni Yoga* 185
[6] *Agni Yoga* 188

refined organism can assimilate the fiery current. Only the fiery heart can unite itself to the Heart of the Cosmos.[1]

Ahamkara—A Sanskrit term meaning a sense of self. The Teacher uses the term in its higher sense. **Ahamkara is the high state of the fiery seed when it can already affirm itself without egoism. Thus the fiery gates are opened when not only is egoism burned away but a worthy evaluation of self is achieved.**[2]

Akasha—A Sanskrit term meaning the all-pervasive *primary energy*-substance of space (ether), the subtlest form of matter. Also see the *Light of Fire*, *Fire Mist*, the *Radiance of the Mother of the World*, and *Materia Lucida*.

Alaya—A Sanskrit turn used in Buddhism to mean primordial awareness, the origin of consciousness. **Lord, in the sacred furnace I will forge the Wings of Alaya.**

Amrita—An elixir of immortality. The highest variety of Amrita or Soma is produced within the organism of the yogi. **Amrita consists of the accumulations of the finest energies.**[3] Also see *Soma*.

Anura—**Perception through the heart bestows a charm that cannot be acquired with gold. The manifestation of Anura—in other words, charm of the heart—is very highly valued. It belongs to among the cumulative and indefinable qualities.**[4]

Arcs of Consciousness—The overlap in consciousness that occurs at a certain stage of communion between the disciple and the Teacher. Also called *Paloria*.

Arhat—An Adept or Initiate of high degree.

---

[1] *Fiery World* III, 174
[2] *Fiery World 1* 602
[3] *Agni Yoga* 207
[4] *Heart* 489

93

Armageddon—A major battle between forces of Light and the forces of darkness. **Certainly the planet is passing through Armageddon, and all its affirmations are sharply divided into camps of Light and darkness.**[1]

Armor. See *Protecting Net.*

Atom—A living organism, life-form or *psycho-life*. It man refer to a tiny atom of physics, a human being, or a cosmic being. The term may have originated from the Egyptian Atum, which has a similar meaning. Also see *Cosmic Atom.*

Attainment—The achievement of selflessness.

AUM—The WORD, the subtle sound of vibrations emanating from the Heart Essence of the Cosmos. The subtle sound emanating from the essential nature of something is its true name.

Aura—The radiation of the energies of the etheric body. Also represents the radiations of the psychic energy of the astral and mental bodies.

Avakara—Fiery inspiration (Sanskrit).[2]

Baptism—Initiation. Also see *Fiery Baptism.*

Battle—**No other word will express that state of inner struggle and success as *battle* does.**[3]

Battle with the Elements. This pertains to the mastery of those elemental forces that we have engendered through our negative thoughts and will. This applies to the karma of humanity as well as the individual. **The Teacher can protect to a certain degree, but the shadow dance of the past will continue its round.**[4]

---

[1] *Fiery World* III, 183
[2] See *Community* 180.
[3] *Heart* 585
[4] *Agni Yoga* 121 also see *Agni Yoga* 121, 122, & 127.

Bee-ness—The Reality beyond words or concepts. Equivalent to the Sanskrit term, Tathata or pure Being. **Be-ness, in its boundlessness, may be affirmed as Infinity.**[1] **Since Be-ness is Fire, all is permeated with it.**[2]

Bhakti Yoga—A path to spiritual union through love and devotion, the mastering of one's emotional nature, and by opening the heart. Agni Yoga includes Bhakti Yoga within it.

Blending of Consciousness—The overlapping of the consciousness of the student with the spiritual consciousness of the Teacher. Also see *Paloria*.

Bodhisattvas—Masters of the spiritual *Hierarchy* who instead of entering the highest nirvana choose to remain in the three worlds of samsara to aid humanity in their evolution. In the Buddhist community Maitreya and Padmasambhava are such.

Brahmarandhara—The twelve-petaled heart center at the crown of the head. In India it is called the 'Gate of Brahma,' and the 'Nirvana Chakra.' It is through this center that the creative *Fire of Space* is condensed as it enters the ethereal body before being naturally distributed to other centers.[3]

Brahmavidya—The doctrine of divine creativeness. Also see the *Fire of Brahmavidya* and *Primal Energy*.

Breath of Cosmos. See the *Breath of the Mother of the World*.

The Breath of the Mother of the World—Streams of cosmic *thought creativeness*, also known as *Rays of the Supermundane Spheres* and *Currents of Evolution*.

The Brotherhood—The *Hierarchy*, the spiritual Community of divine Bodhisattvas who guard and guide the spiritual evolution of the world.

By Thy God—The suggestion to tolerate other people's religion and their approach to the Supreme. **Four prescriptions are given: Reverence to**

---

[1] *Infinity* I, 266
[2] *Infinity* I, 56.
[3] See Agni Yoga 549.

95

Hierarchy, Realization of Unity, Realization of co-measurement, and Application of the Cannon "By thy God."[1]

Call of Space—Distinct is the call of Space; one has only to desire to hear **it.**[2] Also called the *Fiery Impulse*. Also see *Currents of Evolution*.

Cementing Space—To saturate space with creative thoughts that are in step with evolution. **Much can be facilitated by constant calm and affirmative thought directed with intension.** Also see *Thought Creativeness*.

Chalice—A secret center where the incoming fire of Spirit and the yogi's refined psychic energy is stored and used for the common good. In response to communion and the yogi's heart felt striving the Sacred Fire descends into the chalice illuminating of the consciousness. **The gifts of the Higher Forces are gathered in the chalice and given form the chalice.**[3] **Since times immemorial the Chalice has been a symbol of Service…. The symbol of the Chalice has always stood for self-sacrifice. Whoever bears the Chalice bears achievement. Each lofty deed can be marked by the symbol of the Chalice. Everything most lofty, everything for the good of humanity, should bear this symbol. All images of Heroes of the Spirit may be represented as bearing the Chalice.**[4] See *Abramram*.

Co-measurement—To measure one's action in accordance with the event or truth encountered. For example measuring what you say according to the consciousness of your listener. Also applies to measuring the truth with the appropriate measuring stick. Francis Bacon, in his *Advancement of Learning*, writes: "We aught not to attempt to draw down or submit the mysteries of God to our reason; but rather to raise and advance our reason to the divine truth." **Each action can be measured only in accordance with its relation to Hierarchy and Infinity. When we speak of the magnitude of**

---

[1] *Agni Yoga* 570

[2] *Infinity* I, 78.

[3] *The Fiery World* III, 49

[4] *The Fiery World* III. 49

96

fundamentals let us beware of applying earthly measures. Let us especially not base our concepts on the finite because, in essence, the finite does not exist.[1] Earthly measure is not applicable to the grandeur of Cosmos.[2]

Communion—A heart connection with the Teacher, the Hierarchy, the Supreme. It can be initiated through prayer. The highest form of prayer, says the Teacher, is made without words. Silent communion leads to *Paloria*, unity of consciousness.

Community. See *Hierarchy.*

Concatenation—The unification of the parts, as links in a chain. **The concatenation of the universe with all higher spheres should be adopted by the consciousness as a saving anchor in the advancement of the higher foundations of the future.**[3] Concatenation embraces the principle of Hierarchy, the united cosmic link with Infinity.

Concordance—**Concordance is the unifying principle, which affirms the sacred intercourse between spirit and spirit, between spirit and the planet, between spirit and cosmos, between cosmos and the power of the infinite.**[4]

Consciousness of Space—The universal mind.[5] The term space is often used in the Teaching to mean spiritual space. The consciousness of space, for example, is similar to the Sanskrit *Alaya*, primordial awareness.

Containment—The realization of the all-inclusiveness of infinity, nothing real is separated or excluded.[6]

Cosmic Affinity. See *Affinity.*

---

[1] *AUM* 241
[2] *Fiery World III, 44*
[3] *Infinity I*, 23.
[4] See verse 94 above.
[5] See *Agni Yoga* 181 & 218.
[6] See *Infinity* 1. 18

Cosmic Atom—A spiritual being of a level far beyond the human kingdom. Also called *Cosmic Magnet*.

Cosmic Breath. See *Breath of Cosmos* and *Current of Evolution*.

Cosmic Energy. See *Fire of Space* & *Cosmic Fire*.

Cosmic Fire—The fiery essence that permeates all that lives is Cosmic Fire, emanating from the depths of the Cosmos and proceeding into infinite creative manifestations.[1] Also see *Fire of Space* and *Currents of Evolution*.

Cosmic Fusion—That which attracts, unites and holds the universe together. Also called *Concordance*.

The Cosmic Magnet—The Cosmic Magnet is our sacred power. Boundless is the immensity of this Power…. The Arhat proceeds carrying the power of the Cosmic Magnet in his heart.[1]

Cosmic Patterns—The archetypal blueprints of evolution. Also see *Nets of materia lucida* and *Cosmic Seed*.

Cosmic Reason—Universal Mind.

Cosmic Right. See *The Current of Evolution*.

Cosmic Scales. See *Karma*.

Cosmic Seeds—Living archetypal thought-forms that contain the blueprints of evolution. A correspondence of these cosmic seeds are found within each individual. Similar to Plato's Idea-forms (Eidos). See also *Psychic Seeds, Cosmic Patterns, Cosmic Web, Materia Lucida,* and *Web of Materia Lucida*.

Cosmic Solitude—The realization of spiritual union while still in the isolation of physical incarnation. Similar to the Sanskrit term 'Kivalya' (isolated unity).

Cosmic Stream. See '*Current of Evolution*.'

---

[1] *Fiery World* III, 146.

98

Cosmic Thought Frame—The evolutionary pattern upon which the substance of manifestation is built. Also see *Primary Substance* and *Cosmic Web*.

Cosmic Waves—The cyclic patterns produced by the *Currents of Evolution* as they spirals into manifestation from the Higher Worlds.

The Cosmic Web—The subtle structural patterns of manifestation, also called the 'radiant garment of the Mother of the World' and the *Web of Materia Lucida*. In Theosophical teaching it is called the Akashic Web.

Cosmic Whirl. See *Cosmic Waves*.

Creativeness—Through what is the spirit transformed? Through the creativeness of the impulse.[1] The creative impulse is the divine impetus to evolve spiritually. The creativeness of the Knights of the Sacred Fire includes the saturation of space, in cooperation with Hierarchy and the fiery Impulse, with those *psychic seeds*, necessary for creation of a New World.[2] **Creativeness encompasses the fiery potential. It is impregnated with the sacred fire of the heart.**[3]

Crystals of Fohat—See *Crystals of Materia Lucida*.

Crystals of Materia Lucida—Precipitations of psychic energy in either ethereal or dense forms. The physical crystals are looked for and sometimes found at the heart center of great saints during the cremation of their bodies.[4] In Tibet these crystals were called ringsel crystals (*ringse*), Secret Bodhichitta, and Wish-fulfilling Gems. The Rosicrucians called them Philosopher's Stones, as they were stones created within the body of the philosophers. It was highly sought after by the alchemists. They **sharpen the center of the third eye and also serve as the substance for astral construction on the highest plane.** Also called *Ringse, Crystals of Fohat* and *Crystals of Psychic Energy*.

Crystals of Psychic Energy. See *Crystals of Materia Lucida* and *Ringse*.

---

[1] *Hierarchy* 43
[2] See *Fiery World* III 248 & 251.
[3] *Heart* 1
[4] See *The Life of Milarepa*. Translated by Lobsang P. Lhalungpa, Boulder 1984, p.220.

Currents of Karma. See *Karma*.

Currents of Evolution— The driving forces or rays behind cosmic evolution. The quality and keynotes of these divine rays change according to the necessity of the times. The keynotes for the beginning New Era of Maitreya include Beauty, Community, *Hierarchy*, Women, Battle, Synthesis and *Psychic Energy*. Also called the Cosmic Stream, *Rays of Evolution, Fiery Right* and the *Breath of the Mother of the World*.

Currents of Space. See *Currents of Evolution*.

Dare—Fearlessness.

The Densification of the Subtle Body enables yogis to visibly appear where needed in the world in their subtle bodies. Also see also *Divisibility of spirit*.

Dharma—Free will activity that is instep with Evolution.

Direct-knowledge. See *Straight-Knowledge*.

Divisibility of the Spirit—The projection of one's own image and the sending of parts of one's spirit. One should know that simultaneously someone sees this image and receives help.[1] Some initiates, while living in a physical body, are also actively serving upon the higher planes or elsewhere in the world in their subtle body. In India yogis are sometimes seen at more that one location at the same time.

Drops of Grace—A precipitation of the *Sacred Fire* into the *Chalice* producing the 'drops of bliss,' *Amrita,* the elixir of immortality, also known as *Soma*.

Dual Origin—Spirit and Nature, Shiva and Shakti, Purusha and Prakriti.

The Echo of Space—The ever repeating turns of the spiral of life, creating the cyclic rhythm of the evolutionary process.

Education of the Heart—The fine-tuning, through close observation, one's heart sensitivity. **Contact with the subtlest energies refines the entire**

---

[1] *Hierarchy* 92.

being. He who has entered the fiery path understands the refinement, keenness, and vigilance of which I speak. In the education of the heart, unnoticeably to ourselves, we become accustomed to the spheres of the Subtle World. This occurs not because of some exceptional and miraculous phenomena but through minute sensations, which the sensitized heart begins to discern. One must acknowledge the idea of the significance of delicate sensations... Gradually, little by little, we acknowledge that there exists about us a great number of manifestations that cannot be included in the laws of elementary physics. Experiences will increase, and an entire sequence of the sensations of the subtle world will be brought together. This will be the most apparent beginning of the approach to the subtle world.

Epoch of Fire. See *Epoch of Maitreya.*

Epoch of Maitreya—The Age of Aquarius, coinciding with the beginning of *Satya Yuga*, the Age of Truth and Light, which we are at its beginning. The *Kali Yuga*, the Age of Darkness, in now coming to an end. Also called the Epoch of Fire.

Ethereal Body—The subtle energy matrix of the physical body, its prototype, that with nourishes it and gives it life. Also called the etheric body and the double.

The Far-off worlds—Let us regard the far-off worlds— the life there is affirmed in beauty and in striving for achievement; there are the fires of spirit; there is the fire of love; there the seeming excrescence of earth are transformed into creations of fire.[1]

Feminine Origin—Arising from Nature. See *Dual Origins, Mother of the World* and *Materia Lucida.*

Fiery Baptism—Initiation by fire.

Fiery Flame. See *Fire of Space.*

Fiery Guards. See H*ierarchy.*

---

[1] *Infinity* I, 44

Fiery Impulse—The driving motivating force behind cosmic evolution **How important it is to guard the fiery impulse! Without this impelling force an undertaking cannot be saturated with the best possibilities.**[1] When the fiery impulse meets with a spontaneous response the yogi's actions are said to be in step with the *currents of evolution*. Also called Spiritual Will.

Fiery Lotus—See Silver Lotus.

Fiery Medicines—**One must carry out experiments, strengthened by fiery medicines, upon the processes of thinking. One should pay attention to the action of phosphorus or of the evaporation of eucalyptus upon thinking. One should verify the extent to which thinking is improved by musk. One should gather all data in regard to various resinous oils.**[2] One of the best sources of phosphorus is baking soda, which may be takes in small doses dissolved in hot raw milk, which helps to facility its absorption into the nervous system.

Fiery Rays. See *Rays*.

Fiery Striving—**The Joy of the heart lies is striving upward.**

Fiery Right—Activity that is in concordance with evolution. Also see *The Law of Cosmic Right.*

Fiery Thought—**In its timelessness and spacelessness thought belongs to the Subtle World, but still deeper possibilities must also be discerned in this construction. Fiery thought penetrates deeper than that of the Subtle World; therefore fiery thought more truly manifests the higher creativeness. With attention, everyone can distinguish these two strata of thought. During the usual trend of thought we are often conscious of a current, as it were, of a second thought, which clarifies and intensifies the first. This is not a division of the thought, on the contrary, it is a sign that deeper centers have begun an active participation.**[3] One of the best ways to develop fiery thought is by

---

[1] *Hierarchy* 93

[2]

[3] *Fiery World* I #102

102

observing it as it arises within us. Watch for it as a clarification and broadening of the thoughts presented in the Teaching. Also see *Illumination, Psychic energy* and *Thought-creativeness.*

Fiery Warriors are often called by this name because *Satya Yuga* begins with the approach of the element of Fire. Those who gather at this time are imbued with this penetrating element. Also known as The Knights of the Sacred Fire.

Fiery World—The Teaching speaks of three worlds, the 'earthly sphere,' the 'subtle world,' and the highest, the 'fiery world.' The fiery world is without form yet includes consciousness, beauty, splendor and the continued evolution of its inhabitants. The mental plane is mentioned in the Teaching as a bridge between the physical and the fiery world.

Fire—Each of us carries within himself the One Fire, immutable throughout the entire universe. No one cares to imagine that the universal treasure is within him.[1] Also called *Primary Energy, Agni, Cosmic Fire*, the *Fire of Space,* and *Psychic energy.*

Fire Blossom—Symbolizes the lotus of the heart center of the body and of the spirit.

Fire of Brahmavidya—*Agni,* primary psychic energy. Its external manifestation can sometimes be seen with the physical eyes as rainbow *Sparks of Fohat.*

Fire of Infinity. See *Fire of Space.*

Fire of Space—Cosmic Fire and *Sacred Fire.* In response to the yogi's heart felt striving it is precipitated into the *Chalice*, illuminating the consciousness, and stimulating the activity of the centers. The Fire of Space contains the *Fiery Impulse* to evolve spiritually along certain predetermined lines. **When we speak of the Spatial Fire we have in mind those seeds that affirm life and which strain** (propels) **all life forms toward the manifestation of** their destiny. **Certainly, no one doubts that the Fire of Zoroaster is the Fire of Space, which you now study.**[2] **For strengthening the aura not only is**

---

[1] *Fiery World* I # 7
[2] *Agni Yoga* 416

a pure consciousness needed; one must also attract the Fire of Space.[1] Also called *Fohat*, the *Current of Evolution*, and the *Breath of the Mother of the World*. See *Agni*.

Fire of the Heart—The fire of bodhi, heart felt spiritual sensitivity, and the source of wisdom. On a lesser scale it may also refer to the awakened heart center. Also see *Teros* and *Psychic Energy*.

Fire of the Sun. See *Fire of Space*.

Fire-mist—Radiant energy-substance, *Materia Lucida*.

Free energies—The free energies can mold the karma of weak spirits. The space abounds with such tossing spirits.[2] Also see *Elements*.

Fohat—A Theosophical term meaning the *Primal Energy*. See also the *Fire of Space* and the *Fire of Brahmavidya*.

The Formula of Psychic Energy governs the creativeness of thought and its manifestation into form for the sake of the world. It is based upon the idea that the realization of higher truth sets in motion the manifestation of that truth in the material and psychic worlds. The realization of the essential unity of the cosmos, for example, helps to establish this unity in the hearts of the people. To perceive the patterns of energy unfolding on higher levels tends to bring those archetypal energies more closely into manifestation. The formula of psychic energy works through the law of attraction and correspondence by drawing to us those energies that correspond to what we think about and what we strive toward with clarity and intension. Also see *Thought Creativeness*.

Goal Fitness—Activity leading to selflessness, self-perfection, and union with the divine.

Great Service—This great concept of Service is usually completely misunderstood or if accepted at all it is mistaken for monastic monotony. But Great Service responds to earthly needs and the true

---

[1] *Agni Yoga*, 438
[2] *Infinity* I, 369.

servant of humanity must know all conditions of life. He must spare the feelings of the ignorant; he must soothe the desperate, and must appreciate the various fields of labor in order to able to give wise encouragement. In this way service will bring benefit everywhere and the servant of good will know how to find the word that will lead people to a new, luminous age. In the Mysteries it was called the 'Great Work' and the 'One Work.'

Guardians of Humanity. See *Hierarchy*.

The Guiding Star—Karma is the guiding star, affirmed by the actions of many lives… The guiding star will be that skiff which conveys one to the other shore amid the raging elements.[1] K*arma*, divine justice, is beneficial for it teaches us responsibility by forcing us to experience the effects of irresponsibility. Through the guiding star of karma we can begin to understand the true direction of the evolutionary process.

Golden Network—An intricate weave of ethereal nadi that form the foundation of the *chalice*.

The Great Pilgrim—The Christ.

The Great Work—Labor, in cooperation with the *fiery impulse* of the Hierarchy, that furthers the evolution of consciousness.

Hatha Yoga intensifies the separate centers. It can only be regretted that these partial endeavors do not lead to *Raja Yoga* and *Agni Yoga*.[2]

Heart—A refined heart-felt spiritual sensitivity, above the levels of desire and self-centered emotion, that encompasses both love and wisdom. Heart is always expressed in relation to others and to the greater whole, but not in relation to oneself. **How necessary it is to learn to feel one's heart as not one's own but as the universal One. Only through this feeling can one liberate oneself from egotism.**[3] **The heart, is the sun of the organism,**

---

[1] *Fiery World* III, 82
[2] *Fiery World* I, 13.
[3] *Heart* 7

the focus of psychic energy. It is beautiful to sense the heart as the Sun of Suns of the Universe.[1]

Heart of the World. See *Hierarchy*.

Heart-Striving—The power of thought depends upon calmness and heart-striving. This should always be kept in mind, because people too often place the will in the brain.[2]

The Hierarchy—Masters of Wisdom, the Elder Brothers of Humanity, *Bodhisattvas* who guard and guide the spiritual evolution of the world. **Let words about the Lords resound in all corners of the world. They are candles lit before the holy shrines. They are lamps of Living Fire—a protection against all diseases.**[3] Also called *The Brotherhood*, the *Guardians of Evolution, Cosmic Magnet,* Friends of the Earth, Fiery Guards, Heart of the World, and Servants of the Cosmos.

Higher Will—The Way of Spiritual Evolution. **The entire cosmic significance of the Higher Will should be understood.**[4]

Higher Worlds—The spiritual worlds. Also known as the *Spheres of the Infinite* and the *Far-off Worlds*. See also *Fiery World*.

Illumination—**The Fiery World brings us flashes of illumination, similar to lightning flashes in the course manifestation of a thunderstorm. Just as storms always supply Earth with a purified store of prana, so does the Fiery World constantly pour out waves of influences. It is a pity that the receivers are few, but if one were to begin to exercise the consciousness for a communion with the Fiery World, then such a receiver could become naturally affirmed. But the simplest for all worlds is to adhere firmly to Hierarchy.**

Imperil—Crystalized negative deposits of psychic energy in the nerve endings produced from irritation at the imperfections in the world. A correspondence

---

[1] *Heart* 2
[2] *Brotherhood* 546
[3] Fiery World I 10
[4] Hierarchy 286

of it can remain in the subtle body of the individual even after death. It is the negative counterpart to the precipitation of *psychic energy,* called *Rinse* and the *Crystals of Materia Lucida,* which are produced in the subtle and even the physical body of the yogi as a pure manifestation of spiritual exaltation and bliss.

Infinity—Infinity is the great unembellished and indestructible Reality. Also see *Be-ness.*

Inner Lotus. See the *Chalice.*

Justice of Space See *Spatial Justice.*

Kalachakra—A highly veiled esoteric teaching, which according to legend, was given by the Buddha to the King of *Shambhala.* **I approve of the Kalachakra, now being compiled. This fiery Teaching is covered with dust, but it should be proclaimed. Not reason but wisdom gave this Teaching. It should not be left in the hands of ignorant exponents. Many domains of knowledge are united in the Kalachakra; only the unprejudiced mind can find its way among these stratifications of all worlds.**[1] Though the original Kalachakra text has been lost an abbreviated version called the Kalachakratantra, which was written by a latter Shamballa king, is available in Sanskrit, Tibetan, and Mongolian translations. Vasna Wallace is presently translating it from these three languages into English along with its 'Great Commentary' the Vimalaphrbha. As of this writing two of the five chapters have been translated into English and are available in book form. The subjects of this exalted teaching include, Esoteric Astrology, Initiation, the Practice, Wisdom, and the Law of Correspondence between the subtle (vajra) body, the human kingdom, and the spiritual.

Kali Yuga—The Age Darkness. According to the Teaching we are now at the end of the *Kali Yuga,* the Age of Darkness, and the beginning of *Satya Yuga,* the Age of Truth. **Anyone who knows about the approaching end of the Kali Yuga understands that it cannot occur without world upheavals. The forces that were particularly powerful during the 'Black Age' must now struggle**

---

[1] *Fiery World* I. 212

for survival, and they prefer general catastrophe to defeat.[1] One can only hope that the end of the Kali-Yuga does not turn into The End![2]

Karma is the effect of the creative energy and activity of thought, which continues to live on in space, attracting corresponding energies and events. Technically karma is generated by the free will thoughts that are not in harmony with the flow of evolution. Dharma,[3] on the other hand, is the creative activity of thought that is in harmony with evolution. It is for this reason that the Buddha's teaching was called dharma. **Consider thought as a creator**.[4] The responsibility for the creativeness of our thoughts is enforced by karma. Also see *Guiding Star*.

Karma in relation to time. The Teaching distinguishes between two types of karma, individual personal karma and karma that is related to a particular time. Time karma is the result of mental activity that produces obstructions of a predestined event. This usually applies to group, national or world karma.[5]

Karma Yoga—The path to spiritual union through right activity, particularly the activity of thought that is instep with the current of evolution. Agni Yoga includes Karma Yoga. See *Labor*.

Kernel of the Spirit. See *Seed of the Spirit*.

Knights of the Sacred Fire—The spiritual warriors of *Rigden*, the Coming Avatar, to which the Teacher is closely associated. Also called *Fiery Warriors*.

Kriyashakti. See *Psychic Energy*.

Ketub—Another name for the *fire of the heart*.

---

[1] *Supermundane*, 127
  [2] *Heart* 474
[3] Dharma as the term is used in Buddhism, is an abbreviation Buddha-dharma, the Way as taught by the Buddha.
[4] *Infinity* I, 3
[5] See *Agni Yoga* 391

Labor—When I speak of awareness of labor I mean the illumination bestowed through conscious toil.[1] Illumination arises through labor that is in step with the Way because it unites the consciousness with the Will of the Supreme. As a path it is called *Karma Yoga*.

Lamp of the desert—A level of illumination and service where the inner light of the yogi becomes a beacon of salvation for those living on the desert of the physical plane.

Law of Causality—Due to the unity and interconnectedness of the cosmos and the creativeness of thought, every thought, has its effect in the world. With this as our understanding we can greatly enhance our *thought creativeness* for the common good. **How beautiful is the law that gives life to every good and each creative beginning.** The Law of Causality also governs the effects that the *Current of Evolution* has upon the world, effects that enter life through the *cosmic chain* that links each higher cause with each corresponding manifestation. This law also governs the negative effects caused by the freewill of man when creating causes that are not in harmony with the flow of evolution. In this it is often called the *law of karma*.

Law of Cosmic Right—This law governs the freewill activity of humanity in relationship with the Way. Also see *Karma*.

Law of Goal-fitness. See *Goal-fitness*.

Law of Equilibrium. See *Karma*.

Law of Karma—The law that governs the effects of human activity, especially the activity of the thought, in relation to forces of Evolution. **Thus, in former days one was aware of caution during thinking. A grievous thought hangs in the atmosphere,[2] waiting to manifest as a karmic effect. It is karma, the fatiguing aftereffect of previous incarnations that can bring not very savory fellow travelers to us. But when each encounter is over, there comes relief, as when property belonging to others has been returned. No less than half of all earthly encounters take place because of past incarnations, in the way that cork figures are drawn**

---

[1] *AUM* 477.
[2] *Heart* 161

together by application of electrical energy. The broad influence of karma brings about many complicated levels and degrees of relationship. To resolve them, it is better to pay than to receive; for each payment terminates a debt from the past, whereas receiving binds one again.[1] Also see *Karma.*

Law of Fire governs and maintains the creative Impulse to evolve spiritually. Also see *Fiery Impulse.*

Light—Radiant energy.

The Light of Abhidharma—The Sacred Fire, which includes psychic energy and the Fire of Space.

The Light of Fire—The radiance of the all-pervading Cosmic Fire. Also called the *Radiance of the Mother of the World,* and *Materia Lucida.*

The Light of the Chalice—A radiant light emanating from the psychic energy of the Chalice. In Sanskrit it is called *Jyotis,* the Light in the Head, seen by yogis in Meditation. See *The Yoga Sutras of Patanjali* 3: 25.

Light-mindedness—The inability to take life seriously, in particular the the importance of the Teaching and applying the it in life. **Light-mindedness is a world wide failing![2]**

The Lion of the Desert—A degree of self-mastery where the initiate applies will, daring and courage in selfless labor for the common good upon the desert of the physical plane.

Lotus—A center in the subtle body or higher.

Lotus of Cosmos. See *Cosmic Magnet*

The Luminaries—The *Far off Worlds* of the heavens. Also called *Cosmic Magnets.*

---

[1] *Agni Yoga 238*
[2] *Agni Yoga 399*

The Luminary—The Magnet of the Sun. This is not the physical sun but rather the spirit or essence behind it. In the Mysteries it was called the 'Spiritual Sun'.

Magnet of Infinity. See *Cosmic Magnet.*

Magnets—Radiant beings, either human or cosmic. Can also refer to a magnetized objects or images.

Mahavan—A highly refined rhythmic vibration, sometimes sent to a disciple as a protection. May be a simplified spelling of the Sanskrit term mahavahan meaning 'great (*maha*) vehicle (*vahan*)'

Maitreya—A disciple and close childhood friend of the Buddha, who instead of entering the highest nirvana remained in our planetary sphere to aid in the liberation of humanity form the bondage of ignorance. The Buddha proclaimed him as his successor, the next Buddha. Some Buddhist scriptures prophesy that he will appear to the world within the next two to three hundred years. Theosophists identify him with the Christ.

Mantra—The power of mantra lies not in the physical sounds but with the subtle sounds produced by rhythm of thought together with the realization of the inner meaning of the words.

Materia Lucida—Luminous substance. The alchemists called it prima materia or first matter, the fire-mist from which the phenomenal world is woven, and a subtle manifestation-crystallization of *psychic energy*. Also known as the *Radiant Principle*, *Materia Matrix*, and the *Radiance of the Mother of the World*. The Theosophists call it *Akasha*.

Materia Matrix—The essential nature of the material universe. **Psychic Energy is both Fire and Materia Matrix.**[1] See *Materia Lucida.*

Maya is a Sanskrit term meaning the illusion of physical plane existence. **The illusion of life is created only by thought, which limits the cosmic expressions.**[2] It is a mistake to label maya as unreal or not existing. A movie

---

[1] *Agni Yoga*, 416
[2] *Infinity* I, 45

111

is not real life and should not be taken as such, but it's a real movie. It is only an illusion when it is not perceived correctly; the illusion is in the mind not in its substantial nature.

Medium—Open centers are symptoms of right development, but with them comes the danger of mediumism. A medium is but an inn for disembodied liars.[1]

Mental Energy—*Psychic Energy.*

Mental World—Observe that in enumerating the worlds we seem to omit the world of thought. This is not by accident. The Mental World constitutes a living link between the Subtle and Fiery Worlds.[2]

Mind of Cosmos—Universal Mind.

Moksha—A Sanskrit term meaning the liberation from the limitations of ignorance and the material world.

Monad—The Greek sages used to term to mean any whole system or organism, including the ONE itself.

Mother of Agni Yoga—Helena Roerich, also know as *Urusvati* and *Tara.*

The Mother of the World—The Mother of the World is *Shakti*, the all pervading *Primary Energy*, the fiery livingness of all nature as well as the energy substance from which arises the phenomenal universe. "One should learn to accept the fiery nature of all that exist."[3] She is Mother Nature, who with divine intelligence coordinates and gives life and substance to the grounds through which Evolution unfolds. **From time immemorial the Mother of the World has sent forth to achievement. In the history of humanity, Her Hand traces an unbreakable thread. On Sinai Her Voice rang out. She assumed the image of Kali. She was at the basis of the cult of Isis and Ishtar. After Atlantis, when a blow was inflicted upon the cult of the spirit, the Mother of the World began to weave a new thread, which will now begin to radiate. After Atlantis the Mother**

---

[1] *Agni Yoga 228*
[2] *Fiery World* I, 84
[3] *Supermundane 928*

112

of the World veiled Her Face and forbade the pronouncement of Her Name until the hour of the constellations should strike. She has manifested Herself only partly; never has She manifested Herself on a planetary scale.[1]

Nerve Centers—Subtle nerve plexuses of the ethereal body called charkas or wheels of fire. Also known as *magnets*.

Net of Protection. See *Protecting Net*.

The Nets of Materia Lucida—Interconnecting networks of subtle currents of light (radiant energy), providing the inner structure and archetype for the phenomenal universe. Sometimes called the Akashic Web.

New World—As Moses brought forth human dignity, the Buddha impelled toward the broadening of consciousness, the Christ taught the good of giving, so now the New World is directed toward the far-off worlds![2] Already the lightning of a New World illuminates the horizon.[3]

Ojas—*psychic energy*.

Origins. See *Two Origins*.

Outer Lotus—A fiery armor that surrounds and protects the yogi. It is produced as a reflection of the *Inner Lotus* and the rotation of the Kundalini through the *nerve centers*. Also see the *Shield* & *Protecting Net*.

Paloria—The unity of the individual consciousness with the spiritual consciousness. One of the steps toward this is an overlapping of the yogi's consciousness with the consciousness of the Guru. Also called *Unity of Consciousness*. See *Agni Yoga* 563.

Paranirvana—The highest nirvana.

---

[1] *Leaves of Morya's Garden* 2, 220
[2] *Community 81*
[3] *Leaves of Morya's Garden* 2, 259

Paths of the Spatial Fire. Also called 'Rays of Supermundane Spheres,' *'Current of Evolution'* and *'Thread of the Fire of Space.'*

Philosopher's Stone—The Philosopher's Stone, as a physical accumulation of psychic energy, is at the foundation of all life.[1] **The Philosopher's Stone is something real. It can be understood both spiritually and physically. The spiritual state that is called "the Stone" corresponds to a harmonious blend of all the deposits of psychic energy. Physically speaking, this preparation is quite close to a preparation of Paracelsus.** See *Ringse.*

Phosphorus—A luminous substance that strengthens the nerves and nourishes the all-pervading fires of *Soma* in the body. A good source for phosphorus is soda-bicarbonate, which may be taken with hot raw milk for better assimilation. Cod-liver oil also promotes assimilation. **One should guard the fire as a treasure. The phosphorus of the nerves is being consumed as a wick; and is the lamp fit without it? One can add the oil of ozone, but without the wick the nerves will not kindle the fire. One should remember about soda not only in sickness but also in health. As a bond with fiery actions, it serves as a shield against the darkness of destruction. But one should accustom the body to it gradually. Each day it should be taken with water or milk, and in taking it one should, as it were, direct it into the nerve centers.** Also see *Soma.*

The Pledge—The pledge is made before Hierarchy to labor for the sake of the world, to aid in the Great Work of Spiritual Evolution. **Once the pledge is pronounce it becomes the foundation of karma. . . . The pledge is a manifestation of tremendous significance. It creates a chain of hearts and turns chaos into conscious arteries of space.**[2] The pledge is also given to stand by, guide, and even protect one's disciples. Do not pronounce the pledge unless you are ready to accept the responsibility.

Podvig—Spontaneous heroic activity, often involving great courage and personal sacrifice.

Power of Thought—*Psychic Energy.*

---

[1] *Agni Yoga 495*
[2] See *Hierarchy* 299-300 & *Heart* 46

114

Pralaya—A Sanskrit term meaning the absorption or abstraction of the universe into the core essence of Be-ness, causing the destruction of the external universe. Pralaya is to the cosmos what *paranirvana* is to the yogi.

Primal Energy—All that exists is imbued with primal energy.... It should be recognized that the energy of thought (psychic energy) is one of the highest manifestations of primal energy. It is impossible to isolate thought from the fundamental energy of the Cosmos.[1] Also called *Shakti, Fire of Space* and *Agni.*

Primary Matter—As is known, Primary Matter itself—*Materia Matrix*—does not penetrate to the earthly sphere because of the whirling of the infected lower layers. But the so-called Fohat, which is the granulation of Primary Matter, can reach the earthly in the form of sparks and can even be discerned by some eyes when a ray of sunlight crosses the planetary ray, coloring the sparks according to the chemical composition of the ray. Also see *Primary Substance.*

Primary Substance—Before him the weaver has his warp, without which the most skilled craftsman cannot reveal his creative thought. For creativeness of thought, the cosmic thought-frame is also necessary; for thus we name the primary substance from which fiery thought strikes the spark of creation.[2] See *Primary Matter, Akasha, Materia Matrix,* and *Materia Lucida.*

Protecting Net—A shield of light produced through accumulation of *psychic energy* in the *chalice* and projected from there to the extremities. 'Surround yourself with Fire and become immune,' is a most ancient covenant. But, having grown more callous, people began to forget what fire was indicated by the wise. The fire became a physical one and magic circles of fire made their appearance. Thus, people always belittle their essential nature. Actually any living fire is a healing one but no resin can compare with the fire of the heart.[3] The substance of fiery immunity was described by Zoroaster. He pointed out that from each

---

[1] *Supermundane* 213.
[2] *Heart* 50
[3] *Fiery World* 1, 15

115

pore of the skin people could call forth fiery rays to smite all evil. A man clad in a protective armor cannot succumb to any contagion. One can increase this resistance through unity with Hierarchy. Thus, the heart becomes like a sun reducing all microbes to ashes.[1] Also called *The Shield of Teros*.

Psychic Energy—Agni, the Sacred Fire, manifesting in the human kingdom as the creative power of thought, the fire of the heart, and the energies of the centers (prana). The attainment of a strong store of refined psychic energy is called Virya in Sanskrit, one of the Six Perfections of the Buddha. In the same way that matter is now perceived by scientist to be nothing but energy so we should understand the human psychic as essentially subtle energy. Also see *Teros* and *primary energy*.

Psychic Energy of Space. See *Fire of Space*.

Psychic seeds—Creative thought-forms that conform to some aspect of spiritual evolution. They can be of either cosmic or human origin. In the Teaching they usually refer to those living thought-forms created by the yogi and projected into space to hasten the evolutionary process. Cosmic psychic seeds are the living archetypal thought-forms given as the *Fiery Impulse* behind the evolution of consciousness. Plato called them Eidos, divine idea-forms. See Agni Yoga 633.

Psychism—Channeling. **Psychism is a window into the Subtle World, but the teacher tells the pupil, 'Do not turn so often to the window. Look directly into the Book of Life.'[2] Much has already been said about psychism; nevertheless this scourge of humanity is insufficiently understood. Psychism blunts each aspiration, and higher attainment remains inaccessible.... Creativeness is blunted, and there is established a passive state which makes a man an instrument for all kinds of forces. By reason of relaxation of the will, control is weakened, and by this the attraction of various lower entities is increased."[3]**

---

[1] *Fiery World* I, 17
[2] *Fiery World* 2. 14
[3] *Fiery World* 3, 309

Psycho-activity—The sensitive response to cosmic vibrations. **Each vibration evokes the kindling of the centers. Each striving calls forth a cosmic vibration. This resounding we call psycho-activity.**[1]

Psycho-dynamic Force—That which consciously unifies and coordinates spirit-creativeness with the current of evolution.

Psycho-life—A living organism. This includes all life-forms from elemental and atomic lives to the great *Cosmic Magnets* of the heavens. Also see *Atoms*.

Psycho-vision—Clairvoyance.

Radiance of the Mother of the World. See *Materia Lucida*.

Radiant Principle. See *Materia Lucida*.

Raga Yoga—A path to union with the divine through mastery of the mind. Raga Yoga, which is included within Agni Yoga, is based upon the *Yoga Sutras* of Patanjali.

Ray of Silence. See *Agni Invisibilae*.

Rays of the Supermundane Spheres—Streams of cosmic energy that enter our sphere from the cosmic sources. They contains the *Fiery Impulse* behind the evolution of the world. Also called Rays of Evolution, *Currents of Evolution*, and Rays of the far-off worlds.

Reason. See *Cosmic Reason*.

Religare is bestowed on humanity in the form of a religion for unification, for the development of community, for the avowal of the Primary Source. It contains all principles of Being and creates all substances for good.[2]

Rigden—The Coming Avatar. In the Kalachakra he is knows as Rigden Dragpo (or Jyepo), also known as Kalki Rudracakrin, the coming avatar who

---

[1] *Infinity 1*, 245
[2] *Infinity* I, 23.

117

will lead his *Fiery Warriors* into battle against the dark forces. Rigden and the Teacher are very closely associated. **One should gather all unwaveringness of the heart in order to find oneself in the ranks of Rigden.**[1]

Ringse—Sediments of psychic energy, consisting of subtle energies that have been chemically transformed in the organism.[2] Ringse is a Tibetan term, which is spelled Ringsel, (*Sarira* in Sanskrit). It pertains to the pearls colored crystals formed in the body of great yogis. In Tibet they were often found in the ashes after the cremation of the body of a high lama or mahasiddha.[3] **The Tibetan 'ringse' has a deep significance, being the sediment crystallized by the manifestation of bliss.**[4] In the Teaching they are also called 'deposits of psychic energy,'[5] 'crystals of psychic energy,' and 'crystals of *Materia Lucida*.' It Tibet they are called the 'secret bodhichitta' and 'bliss relics' (anandasarira), because of the qualities of consciousness necessary to produce them. In many eastern countries including India, Tibet, China, and Japan these crystals were preserved in secret in stupas, which were created for this purpose. The radiation of these crystals have a powerful effect upon those within their immediate vicinity including the power to spontaneously heal the body and the psyche. They have been called 'Wish-Fulfilling Gems,' as they are said to magnify the power of the striving of those in the immediate proximity. Their existence was kept secret in Tibet up to the time of the Chinese invasion. The Rosicrucians called these crystals '*Philosopher's Stones*,' though this term also includes the radiant source of these crystals. **There is the crystal of universal power, the Philosopher's Stone. Here, once again, the alchemists are close to the truth. The Philosopher's Stone, as a physical accumulation of psychic energy, is at the foundation of all life.**[6] It is a lower correspondence to what is called in the Teaching the **Stone from the far off worlds**, also known as the 'Flaming Diamond.' **On the path to the Fiery World it is necessary to realize those fiery batteries that are contained in man.**[7] **We consider it a treasure when the heart is ever ready to respond to the environment,**

---

[1] *Heart*, 380
[2] *Fiery World* III # 218
[3] See *The Life of Milarepa*. Translated by Lobsang P. Lhalungpa, Boulder 1984, page 220.
[4] *Hierarchy*, 422 Also see Heart, 120 & 354
[5] *Heart*, 120
[6] *Agni Yoga*, 495
[7] *Fiery World* III # 218

being already without tension. It is not easy to do this unless the energies are transformed into resounding crystals. Then there will be formed the Ringse so correctly pointed out in Tibet in the Covenant of the Himalayas.

Sacred Fire—See *Agni, The Fire of Space* & *Primal Fire*.

Sacred Pledge. See *Pledge*.

Samyama—A primary method of Raja Yoga involving one pointed concentration on some question until realization is attained. It is based upon the truth that psychic energy follows thought, that whatever we place our attention upon is thereby stimulated. The principles of samyama are dealt with extensively in Book III of the *Yoga Sutras of Patanjali*, the primary source book for Raja Yoga.

Sangha—An Ashram or Community.

Sangha of Maitreya—The Ashram or Brotherhood of Maitreya the coming Buddha. All the Agni Books are sealed with this inscription in Tibetan.

Satya Yuga—The Age of Truth. According to the Teaching we are now approaching the end of the *Kali Yuga* or dark age and the beginning of Satya Yuga, also known as Krita Yuga and the *Epoch of Maitreya*.

Seed of the Spirit—The spiritual essence within all beings. In the human kingdom it has been called, Atma, Buddha Nature, and Christos. Like all seeds they contain the archetypal blueprints and *fiery impulse* behind their evolution and future perfection. Also see *Monad*.

Seeds of Karma. See *Karma*.

119

Sensar—An ancient esoteric language taken from the subtle geometry of nature and used by the *Hierarchy* in their creative work and to communicate with coworkers in the field. See SENSA: The Secret Language of the Gods, Pentarba Publications.[1]

Serpent Solaris—An aspect of the energy of the Solar Plexus center, which when fully awakened transports the yogi in consciousness to the heavenly realms. Also called the Heavenly Dragon.

Service—See *Great Service.*

Shakti—*Primary Energy.*

Shambhala—Abode of the *Hierarchy.* Also called the *Stronghold.*

Shield—*Protecting Net.*

Shield of Teros—A protecting net of psychic energy. **The essential thing is to summon Teros out of the Chalice to the extremities.**[2] Teros is the *Fire of the Heart.* See *Protecting Net.*

The Shifting of the Currents—The transition between the old world of Kali Yuga and the new world of Satya Yuga requires a shifting of the spiritual currents of evolution. This pertains to a radical **change of direction**, as new incoming energies take the place of old no longer needed energies. The shifting extends to all the currents of life on earth, including elemental and subterranean currents. **The planetary focus, as a manifestation of the** Cosmic **Magnet, is shifting. When the change of energies occurs, not only are the parts shifted but also the entire orbit is involved in this shifting.**[3] Before the New World can arise properly a total **reconstruction of the world** is needed.

Silence. See *Voice of Silence* and *Ray of Silence.*

Silvery Lotus—The radiant formation of the *chalice* that occurs at a certain degree of yoga. **The Silvery Lotus of the fiery heart is not often**

---

[1] Pentarba.com
[2] *Agni Yoga* 565
[3] *Infinity 1*, 359

manifested, even to lofty spirits. But separate petals of the fiery Lotus can be seen, and in accordance with them let us assemble the entire flower. But if this fiery wonder is even once evoked, and viewed by the heart, then from that hour the heart's path leads upward, toward eternal attainment.[1]

Sixth Race—According to H. P. Blavatsky the forefront of humanity are manifesting bodies of the Fifth Race. The Sixth Race is said to begin in approximately 4000 years. It will be established by those pioneers of the spirit who are now beginning to embody the new currents of evolution.

Solar Plexus—The center of the solar plexus gives equilibrium to the all the bodies. Its radiations saturate also the ethereal body, which feed the astral body.[2]

Solar Ray. See *Currents of Evolution.*

Solar Serpent. See *Serpent Solaris.*

Solaris. See *Serpent Solaris.*

Solemnity—The radiance of solemnity indicates the highest achievement of the heart.[3] Solemnity combines in itself ecstasy, ascent, a defense against evil, and the turning toward Hierarchy. Thus solemnity is a salvation, but it must be absorbed and maintained.[4]

Solitude—The Spirit of Darkness, pondering how to still more firmly lash humanity to the Earth, thought: "Let them keep their old customs and habits. Nothing binds humanity so much as habitual forms. But this is fit only for the multitudes. Far more dangerous to us is solitude, in which the consciousness is illumined and new forms are created. Therefore, time in solitude must be severely limited. People must not be allowed to remain alone."

---

[1] *Fiery World II,* 469.
[2] *Fiery World* III, 219
[3] *Heart* 491
[4] *Heart* 525

121

Soma—A Sanskrit term meaning an elixir of immortality. It is produced through the crystallization of psychic energy in the organism of the yogi/alchemists. In many legends, of both the east and the west, the elixir is contained in the sacrificial cup or grail. Maitreya, the coming Buddha, is usually portrayed as carrying the elixir in a vase to be given to those who will accept full responsibility for its use. The term is also used in the Teaching as the name of a corresponding substance found in certain plants, such as *phosphorus.* "Soma makes a new man of the initiate." writes Blavatsky, "He is reborn and transformed, and his spiritual nature overcomes the physical; it bestows the divine power of inspiration, and develops the clairvoyant faculty to the utmost." Also called *Amrita.* See the book, A Synthesis of Alchemy, An inquiry into the Philosophy of Hermetic Philosophy. Pentarba Publication.[1]

Space—Spiritual Space. **All reality is built according to the laws of Space.**[2]

Spatial Justice—Divine Justice, *Karma.*

Spatial Thought—Thought forms originating from the spiritual or universal Mind saturating space with the *Fiery Impulses* pertinent to the evolution of the times. **We take care about broadening the consciousness in order that union with spatial thought may be approached. This must be accepted as simply as is the vital importance of oxygen.**[3] What oxygen is for the body, spatial thought is for the soul. In the Hermetic writings the Eagle was a symbol for both Oxygen and spatial thought. Also called *Currents of Wvolution, Spirit Creativeness, Thought Creativeness* and *Psychic-Seeds.*

Sparks—Colored sparks of light, precipitations of psychic energy, which appear unexpectedly before the vision of the yogi. They are one of signs of Agni Yoga and indicate the accumulation of psychic energy within the centers. They arise **when sufficient sensitivity of the organism has been developed.**[4] They are sometimes sent by the Teacher as a warning or confirmation. Pay attention to your thoughts at such a time. They may also give emphasis to a word or thought while reading. **Where colored sparks**

---

[1] Pentarba.com
[2] *Agni Yoga 243*
[3] *Agni Yoga 363*
[4] Agni Yoga 139

appear, the door is open to the chain of benefaction.[1] As is known, Primary Matter itself—*Materia Matrix*—does not penetrate to the earthly sphere because of the whirling of the infected lower layers. But the so-called *Fohat*, which is the granulation of Primary Matter, can reach the earthly in the form of sparks and can even be discerned by some eyes when a ray of sunlight crosses the planetary ray, coloring the sparks according to the chemical composition of the ray.[2] In the *Kalachakra*, an esoteric scripture taught by the Buddha to the king of *Shamballa*, these rainbow colored sparks, called 'tigle stongpai sgron-ma,' arise spontaneously at a certain level of spiritual development.

Spatial Fire. See *fire of space*.

Spheres of the Infinite. See *far-off worlds*. Also know as *Higher Worlds*.

Spiral of the Life Principle—All life expresses itself as energy. All energy moves forward in a spiral. All cyclic activity follows this principle, including the evolution of consciousness. See *Wheel of Cosmos*.

Spirit-creativeness—The power of thought projected into space for the purpose dissolving of the darkness of human thinking or to build living thought-forms of higher truth corresponding to our present stage of evolution. Also see *Thought Creativeness* and *Psychic-Seeds*.

Spirit-knowledge. See *Straight-knowledge*.

Star of the Mother of the World—The sun.

Straight-knowledge—Spiritual Insight, Enlightenment. **The realization of enlightenment may be defined as straight-knowledge.[3] Not education, not experience, not talent, but precisely the fire of straight-knowledge open the direct path to Shambhala.**

Striving. See *Heart-Striving*.

---

[1] *Hierarchy* 160
[2] *Agni Yoga* 144
[3] *Agni Yoga*, 127.

123

The Stone—A crystallization of *psychic energy* into Akashic, ethereal, or physical energy-substance. See *Ringse*.

Stone from the far off worlds—On the bosom of Earth he will find the Stone from the far off worlds.[1] The legend concerning the Stone or Flaming Diamond as it is sometimes called, tells the story of how the Stone was brought to the earth from a far off world to hasten the evolution of this world. See the *Stone*.

Stronghold—An abode of Hierarchy. Also see *Shambhala*.

Subtle World—The Teaching distinguishes three worlds; the 'earthly sphere,' the 'subtle world,' and the *fiery world*. The subtle world, also called kama-manas, the astral and lower mental plane, is a transitional plane between the earthly sphere and the fiery world. It is where the earthly inhabitants go when the body is discarded.

Summa Summarum—Reconciling the idea of the finiteness of the universe with that of the principle of infinite space.[2] In essence it is Infinite; in manifestation, finite. In essence it is One, in manifestation, many.

Supermundane—Urusvati knows that some people do not understand the difference between the Subtle World and the Supermundane. It seems to them that both concepts are interchanged in our discourses, simply to avoid repetition. But it should be remembered that the Subtle World is a particular and limited realm, while the Supermundane World includes not only the various spheres, but also the world of thought– even the thought produced by those on Earth. It can even be stated that the Supermundane World is mainly the world of thought.[3]

Supermundane Currents. See *Currents of Evolution*.

Supermundane Spheres. See *Far-off Worlds*.

Svati. See *Urusvati*.

---

[1] *Agni Yoga,*
[2] *Agni Yoga,* 91
[3] *Supermundane* III, 642

Synthesis—Essential unity of the whole. **Humanity can be divided into those who accept synthesis and those who deny it. Those who deny the benefit of synthesis do not recognize the history of the human race, where epochs of upliftment were also the epochs of an understanding of synthesis. Please do not think that specialization makes the glory of an era.**[1] Synthesis unifies; analysis divides and separates. Synthesis means *essential* unity and not merely the sum of its parts. The synthesis of the seven colors, for example, is the white light from which they arise. **He who can understand synthesis can understand Hierarchy.** [2]

Tactica Adversa—Using adversity as an aid to the path. By matching one's strength against a strong opponent we grow stronger. **I rejoice if you understand that obstacles are really opportunities.**[3] **When your step is firm, the counterforces are beneficial.**[4]

Tamas—One of the three gunas or qualities of the life process. At their highest level they pertain to the three levels of the Sacred Fire. Tamas is the lowest, the vital or life energy (prana) of the body.

Tara—A name given by the Teacher to Helena Roerich. She is also known as *Urusvati* and the *Mother of Agni Yoga.*

The Teacher—Master Morya, the author of the Agni Yoga Teaching.

The Teaching—The Agni Yoga Books, published by the Agni Yoga Society.

Thought-creativeness—Through the realization that thought creates a powerful field of service can be created.

Tension—Tension, as the term is used in the Teaching, does not refer to the stress of emotional tension or even physical tension, but rather an intensity of psychic energy. **When I indicated tension, I had in mind not muscular tension, but that of the heart.**[5] Pure striving, solemnity, gratitude, and

---

[1] *Supermundane* I, 96
[2] *Hierarchy* 162
[3] *Agni Yoga* 494
[4] *Agni Yoga* 257
[5] *Heart* 186

communion with Hierarchy, all intensify the psychic energy. From this spiritual tension arises the powers and *straight-knowledge* of the saints. **He who has directed his vision toward infinity understands that the higher it is the greater the tension. Thus prepare people for an inevitable intensification.**[1] An intensification of heart energy is necessary to the spiritual Path! When emotional stability is attained this heart tension can become continuous bliss. **The calm of the yogi is as the tension of an ocean wave.**

Teraphim or Teraph—There are two kinds of teraphs, physical and astral. A physical teraph is a sculpted, highly magnetized, image that will provide a link with the one represented in the image. An astral teraph is the same only it is created in the mind through visualization. Both kinds are highly magnetized through the saturation of psychic energy. The image of the Teacher visualized in the third eye and placed in the heart is an astral teraph. **The astral teraph is the product of the crystallization of psychic energy.**[2]

Teros—Psychic energy was sometimes called Teros. In Hermetic writings one may fine this expression: 'The warrior Teros raised his shield.' So was indicated the protective significance of psychic energy. All one's surrounding are subject to the influence of Teros. One can feel the invisible benevolence with which everything responds to the touch of the pure flame.[3] Also called the *fire of the heart*.

The Thinker—Plato. He (the Thinker) **also wrote about Atlantis, but people for a long time regarded it as a myth.**[4] **It is true that Plato knew the power of thought** (i.e. psychic energy), **but he revealed only a clue to its power, because it was dangerous to give this knowledge prematurely to the masses.**[5] **The Thinker was asked why he did not mention the power of thought in his writings. He answered: 'The time will come when humanity will be ready to understand this truth, but each premature transmission will only create obstacles.'**[6]

---

[1] *Heart* 314
[2] *Agni Yoga 419*
[3] *Agni Yoga* 577
[4] *Supermundane 556*
[5] *Supermundane* 99
[6] *Supermundane* 180

Thought-creativeness. See *Creativeness*.

Thread of the Fire of Space—The *current of evolution* and the 'rays of the supermundane spheres'. **The thread of the Fire of Space stretches into Infinity.**

Transformation. See *Transmutation*.

Transmutation—The alchemical process of changing one element or energy-substance into another higher element through the agency of fire (psychic energy). In the Teaching this alchemical process is applied on several levels, physical, human, and cosmic. **When the tensed current of will flows with accelerated speed, matter is absorbed by the spirit and the functions of a spiritual creator are performed. Then the refining of form takes place. The power of the fire of spirit is like the power of fire that melts metals. Only through the process of melting may one form new combinations…. From times immemorial the Lords have assumed the task of melting the consciousness.**[1] The term 'melt' is a veiled reference to the process whereby the energy particles are reduced or transmuted to their original nature and 'matter is absorbed by the spirit' or the consciousness is absorbed into its original state of being.[2]

Two Origins. See *Dual Origins*.

Unity of Consciousness—The consciousness of human beings is basically fragmented. One of the primary goals of yoga is the unification of the consciousness. Also see *Paloria*, which is a very high level of the unification process.

Upasika—The name given to H.P. Blavatsky. See Agni Yoga 141.

Ur—**The root of the Light of Fire. From time immemorial the Radiant Principle has attracted the hearts of many people.**[3] "UR reveals a grand list of shining names. It was in itself the greatest and most likely the original

---

[1] *Infinity* I 24. Also see my *The Gates of Infinity*, which is a commentary on the *Infinity* series. Pentarba.com
[2] See my *A Synthesis of Alchemy: An Inquiry into the Hermetic Philosophy*, Pentarba Publications. Pentarba.com
[3] *Fiery World* I Preface.

127

word for *fire*. The Egyptians, wishing to name it *the* fire, added the divine article, *the*, which in their language was the hieroglyph for the letter P. This addition made it *p-ur, pur*, the Greek word for fire to this day. From this comes *pure, purge, purgatory*, as also *pyre, pyrotechnic* and *empyrean*, the Greek U changing to Y in English, as in hundreds of words. *Ur* (a variant of *aur, or*) was the name of that state of the primordial spiritual fire."[1]

Urominai—The serpent that gnaws at **the forces** of evolution. **Thus, in former days one was aware of caution during thinking. A grievous thought hangs in the atmosphere.**[2] Urominai is the residue of karma, the adverse effects of the energy of negative thinking. It hangs in the atmosphere of its creator awaiting transmutation.

Uru—From the Sanskrit meaning spacious or great. See *Urusvati.*

Urumiya—*Straight-knowledge* that perceives obsession in others.[3]

Urusvati—Helena Roerich, also known as *Mother of Agni Yoga*. Urusvati is a Sanskrit term meaning a great being—Uru means spacious or great; Svati means being (feminine). Ur is giving in the Teaching as the **Light of Fire. Urusvati** is also **the name we have given to the star that is irresistibly approaching the earth. Since long ago it has been the symbol of the Mother of the World and the Epoch of the Mother of the World must begin at the time of Her star's unprecedented approach to the earth. The great epoch is beginning because the spirit understanding is linked with the Mother of the World.**[4]

Valerian—Valerian kindles the fires.[5] **Among the prophylactics against cancer and other fiery ailments one may advise valerian. I often speak of this tonic and preventive remedy, but as with any prophylaxis it must be administered systematically—every evening without fail, like a daily course of the sun.**[6] Valerian Root can be taken as a tea or extract.

[1] Alvin Boyd Kuhn, *The Esoteric Structure of the Alphabet.*
[2] *Heart* 161.
[3] *Fiery World* I, 373.
[4] *Leaves of Morya's Garden* II, 138
[5] *Fiery World* I 381
[6] *Fiery World* I 387

Veil of the Mother of the World—Maya, the appearance of which hides Her essential nature.

Virya—A strong store of highly refined psychic energy. One of the Six-Perfections taught by the Buddha.

Voice of Silence—The essential nature of sound. The Voice Silence is to sound what the white light is to a rainbow of colors. Also called the Silence.

Wings of Alaya. See *Alaya*.